A COMPREHENSIVE GUIDE TO

DEEP
FREEZING

A COMPREHENSIVE GUIDE TO

DEEP FREEZING

by
MORAG WILLIAMS

HAMLYN

LONDON · NEW YORK · SYDNEY · TORONTO

Published by
THE HAMLYN PUBLISHING GROUP LIMITED
LONDON · NEW YORK · SYDNEY · TORONTO
Hamlyn House, Feltham, Middlesex, England

© Copyright Countrywise books 1958
ISBN 0 600 48183 2
Thirteenth edition 1971

Made and printed in Great Britain by
Billing & Sons Limited, Guildford and London

CONTENTS

Introduction 7

Types of Home and Farm Deep Freezers 11

Chest Deep Freezers
Upright Freezers
Where should the Deep Freezer be Placed?
What Size Do You Need?
What does a Deep Freezer Cost to Run?
Looking After the Deep Freezer
Equipment Necessary for Deep Freezing

What to Freeze: How Long and How Much 18

How Long should Food be Deep Frozen?

The Basic Rules 21

Packaging 24

Why Food must be Wrapped
Choice of Packaging Materials
Packaging Materials
Packaging Materials to be Avoided
How to Pack
Sealing
Labelling
Putting Food in the Deep Freezer
Keeping Records

Meat 35

Basic Rules
Packing

Fish 40

Method
Thawing and Cooking

Poultry 43

Method
Thawing and Cooking

Game   47
    Method

Vegetables   50
    Method
    Packing
    Brine Packing
    Freezing
    Directions for Individual Vegetables
    Cooking Frozen Vegetables

Fruit   60
    Method
    Unsweetened Packing
    Dry Sugar Packing
    Syrup Packing
    Headspace Allowances
    Discoloration
    Thawing
    Cooking
    Directions for Individual Fruits

Eggs, Cream, Butter, Ice-cream and Cheese   73
    Packing Eggs
    Thawing Eggs

Bread, Cakes, Sandwiches and Pastry   77

Ready-cooked Foods   82
    General Directions
    Things to Avoid
    Points to Remember

Frozen Food Suppliers   88
Storage "Life" Tables   89
Bibliography   91
Index   92

Introduction

As soon as man began to move on from a kill-and-eat existence—with no thought for tomorrow—he began to devise means of keeping food.

Intelligence prompted food preservation by climatic means. The sun, where it was hot enough, was used to dry; the snow to chill or freeze. Some foods, it was discovered, could be preserved by smoke or salt. Following these natural methods of preservation came the discovery that some foods could be kept in sterile jars and tins. But traditional methods have been limited, either in successful application or because the temperatures which helped to keep the foods were naturally variable, or could not be controlled.

Happily, a method of food preservation has now evolved which extends to a far wider range of food than any of the older methods, and which keeps the colour and flavour of food far better than any traditional method of preservation: food is stored at −5° Fahrenheit and the temperature kept steady at that mark. This method is called *Deep Freezing*.

There's very little doubt that as soon as people realize how successful deep freezing can be, how many more foods can be stored by this new means of preservation, and how quick and simple it is compared to other methods, they will wish they owned a deep-freeze cabinet. They'll begin to ask themselves if they should buy one.

There is no standard economic answer to this question for two priceless factors are involved—convenience and time.

Deep freezing is initially a more expensive method of food preservation than bottling, brining or canning, but it does a better job. Buying a deep freezer is like buying a good vacuum cleaner. There are savings and tremendous gains in efficiency and ease at once.

Deep freezing has most obvious advantages for the food producer. Every garden will produce its glut. The deep-freezer owner can preserve the surplus fruits and vegetables and have them standing by to help the menus through the months when prices rise and variety is hard to find. Meat, poultry, game and fish—foods which cannot generally be preserved by the traditional methods—can all be deep frozen. To the deep-freezer owner "out of season" can become an obsolete phrase.

Those who don't grow their own food must reckon up the costs of buying a deep freezer against the convenience of having a variety of food available and close at hand. They can buy food when it is cheap, and they can minimize the time they have to spend on shopping.

Anyone with a young family can plan against the children's appetites and, instead of baking every other day, or once a week, bake for a month. They can plan and build up for school holidays. Those who entertain can do the same, and spare themselves the tiredness that so often accompanies hospitality.

There's no doubt at all that deep freezing has numerous and well-worth-while advantages.

Naturally there will be some who can't afford to buy a deep-freeze cabinet, but who would still like to be able to preserve food by deep freezing. Even they may have facilities for doing so in the future. Communal deep-freeze plants have been introduced and are spreading throughout the country. If you can't have a deep freezer of your own, you may be able to hire a deep-freeze locker.

Second-hand deep-freeze cabinets are now coming on to the market in quite large numbers. They are of two kinds, the ordinary deep-freeze top-lid opening model and conservator models of the sort you see in shops for storing ice-cream.

It is as well before buying any second-hand cabinet to get a refrigeration engineer to check it thoroughly or to buy from a recognised dealer in second-hand machines.

Types of Home and Farm Deep Freezers

There are two types of domestic deep freezers available, the chest (top opening) freezer and the upright (door opening) model.

CHEST DEEP FREEZERS

Sizes range from 4·2 cu ft to 20·8 cu ft with *gross* storage capacities of 115 lb. to 738 lb. The 13-cubic-foot model being the smallest one which does not carry purchase tax so that in fact the larger sizes are often only a few pounds more than the small ones. *Actual* storage capacities are likely to be less, for the average user will inevitably waste some space by storing irregularly shaped packages. Prices of these freezers range from £57 to £120. The larger models have separate quick-freezing compartments for fast freezing of new additions to the frozen food store.

UPRIGHT FREEZERS

Sizes range from 1·75 cu ft to 20·5 cu ft, with *gross* storage capacities of 50 lb. to 749 lb. Prices range from £43 to £218. Some models have quick-freeze plates for fast freezing new additions.

Both chest and upright freezers work equally well, so the choice depends largely on individual preference. An upright freezer occupies less floor space than a chest model, but larger models should first be tried out for accessibility of stored food. A short person may find it difficult to reach to the back of the top shelves of an upright model. The most inaccessible part of the chest freezer is the bottom of the chest, on the side farthest from the lock. Most chest deep freezers have an arrangement of removable baskets. It is important to see whether these baskets, when fully loaded with food, are within your weight-lifting capacity.

A top-opening chest deep freezer loses less cold air when opened than an upright model, but this loss is unlikely to be significant for a domestic user who will not be opening and closing the lid or door more than once or twice a day.

Remember that the weight of an upright model is very concentrated. Will the floor be strong enough to support it when it is fully loaded?

Chest models can often be placed so that they provide a working surface in the kitchen.

WHERE SHOULD THE DEEP FREEZER BE PLACED?

Space and convenience will, of course, be the real deciders here, but the ideal place is somewhere that is dry, cool and well ventilated.

Dampness may damage both the exterior and the motor.

A hot room will force the motor to run harder to maintain the zero temperature.

Lack of air circulation will result in inefficient removal of heat from the condenser. Deep freezers should *not* be fitted tightly into an old cupboard space.

If the deep freezer is going to be accommodated in the kitchen, keep it as far as possible from any source of heat.

If it is being put into a garage, basement, or pantry, see that the chosen place is dry.

WHAT SIZE DO YOU NEED?

The choice depends on your purse, the size of your family, the likely source of food to be deep frozen (whether it is home-produced or bought), your entertaining, and the turnover of food in the deep freezer.

Because few people pack deep freezers with regularly shaped packets, the calculation of storage capacity is necessarily inexact. *Maximum* storage in pounds per cubic foot is reckoned by multiplying each cubic foot by 30. *Actual* storage capacity in pounds per cubic foot may not be more than cubic feet multiplied by 25. Light-weight food, such as bread, pre-cooked dishes, etc., may further reduce the actual storage capacity.

A guide to capacity is given on p. 19.

Before making the final decision, remember that it may be cheaper in the long run to over-estimate your needs than to buy a deep freezer that will later prove too small. You always lose a great deal when selling electrical equipment second-hand.

WHAT DOES A DEEP FREEZER COST TO RUN?

A number of factors determine running costs—the size of the freezer, its design, the number of times the door or lid is going to be opened and for how long, efficient defrosting, careful chilling of food before it is put into the freezer and, of course, local electricity charges.

A rough, general method of calculating running costs for maintaining zero temperature per 24 hours is:

Size of deep freezer	*Current consumed*
6 cubic feet	0.3 kW. per cubic foot
12 cubic feet	0.25 kW. per cubic foot
18 cubic feet	0.20 kW. per cubic foot

Each manufacturer will give a rough estimate of the current *likely* to be consumed by his machines. The estimates of consumption by the machines at present available are from 1 to 2 units of electricity a day.

LOOKING AFTER THE DEEP FREEZER

Each manufacturer will supply specific directions for the care and maintenance of his deep freezer. The following are general directions only:

Defrosting. Frost which forms around the lid or door of the freezer should be removed frequently. Frost on the walls of the deep freezer does not gravely affect the efficiency of the machine, and defrosting once or twice a year should be sufficient. A good rule of thumb is to defrost when the frost is between $\frac{1}{4}$ and $\frac{1}{2}$ inch thick. If possible, defrost and clean freezer when stocks are low.

Remove the food from the freezer, put it as compactly as possible in a refrigerator, or wrap it in layers of newspaper and place in the coolest place available.

Turn off the current, and scrape off the frost with a plastic or wooden spatula. *On no account should sharp tools or wire brushes be used.* If the deep freezer has no drain, line the bottom with layers of newspaper to catch the frost scraping.

If it has a drain, defrosting can be hastened by resting buckets of hot water in the chest while leaving the lid *open*. Hot water should never be run over the refrigerated surfaces, but, when necessary, cold water may be used to accelerate melting. Before re-packing the freezer with food, let it run for 30 minutes or so.

Cleaning the Deep Freezer. It is convenient to clean the freezer when it is defrosted. Unless specific directions have been supplied with the machine, after defrosting, wash the interior with a solution of warm water and bicarbonate of soda (approximately 1 tablespoonful of bicarbonate of soda to each quart of water). Rinse with clear water and dry thoroughly. Do not use detergents, soaps or caustic cleansers.

Clean the outside of the machine with an enamel surface polish, or according to the manufacturer's specific directions.

The Motor. Specific instructions will be supplied by the manufacturer. Most motors are sealed, and the general direction is to leave well alone, and contact the supplier if anything goes wrong.

Power Failure. Check plug, switch and fuses and if the fault is not domestic, telephone the electricity authority and find out how long the failure is likely to last. If only for a few hours, or even a day, the food inside the freezer should survive without any precautionary action. The fuller the deep freezer with frozen packets, the longer it will stay cool. Depending on the load and insulation, food will keep from 12–72 hours with the power off. But it is well to find out if there is a source of dry ice in the neighbourhood, *before* a crisis. Avoid opening the freezer during power failure unless absolutely necessary. A warning device, bell or light, will indicate if the temperature in the freezer has risen too high. This could happen if the switch had been inadvertently turned off or a fuse blown, apart from there being a power failure.

15 lb. of dry ice in a 6-cubic-foot freezer should protect the food for 2 to 3 days.

Wear thick gloves, and divide the dry ice out into as many pieces as there are storage compartments. Do not put it directly on top of the stored food, but separate the two with paper. Work quickly to avoid loss of cold. Remove only when the current has been restored for a few hours.

EQUIPMENT NECESSARY FOR DEEP FREEZING

After you have bought the deep-freeze cabinet, very little supplementary equipment other than packing materials is needed. The following list gives some useful accessories. Most people will find that they have nearly everything required already:

1. A fine-mesh wire basket with a handle, or a cheese-cloth bag for scalding vegetables.
2. A saucepan or steamer with a lid, large enough to hold the wire basket.
3. A bowl in which the wire basket may be totally immersed.
4. A sharp knife.
5. A spoon and fork (preferably silver) for mixing and crushing fruit.
6. A jug liquid measure.
7. A home-made funnel (remove both ends from a tin) for filling bags.
8. Labelling materials.
9. Packaging materials.

BRITISH DEEP FREEZER
MANUFACTURERS include

British Food Freezers Ltd.,
Birds Eye Ltd.,
Bosch Ltd.,
Electrolux Ltd.,
Esta Freeze Ltd.,
Everest Ltd.,
Frigidaire Ltd.,
Hoover Ltd.,
Hotpoint Electrical Appliance Co. Ltd.,
Kelvinator Ltd.,
Lakeland Plastics Ltd.,
Lec Refrigeration Ltd.,
Philips Ltd.,
Total Ltd.,
Tricity Ltd.,
UPO (U.K.) Ltd.,

Local agents and Electricity Board showrooms can supply full specifications.

AMERICAN AND CONTINENTAL
DEEP FREEZERS

Available from:

Derry & Toms, Kensington High Street, London, W.8
Harrods, Knightsbridge, London, S.W.1.
Heals, 196 Tottenham Court Road, London, W.1
Marshall & Snelgrove, Oxford Street, London, W.1

and other Department Stores.

What to Freeze: How Long and How Much

Nearly all food, except raw salad vegetables, can be preserved satisfactorily in the deep freezer, but after allowing for the first excitement—which will tempt all but the most calm and calculating to have a go at everything—it's wise to pause and think. There is a very dangerous trap called freezing for the sake of freezing.

To bring the problem down to common-sense proportions, is it sensible to freeze more of one food than will be needed to take one on from harvest to harvest, or killing to killing? Of course it's not. Last year's strawberries in the freezer and this year's stawberries in the garden is a maddening experience, but that doesn't mean that it is child's play to avoid it. Crops can fail. That may leave you with "saved" space. The allocation of freezer space calls for more than planning—it needs both planning and some flexibility.

The *selection* of food for freezing is a major part of making the most of your deep freezer, for space is always limited and valuable. There is very little point in freezing meat on any scale if it can be supplied fresh by a near-by butcher unless by buying in quantity considerable saving can be effected. Nor is there any point in freezing gluts of fruits and vegetables that you don't like. The deep freezer should be used to preserve foods that all the family enjoy. It should be used to preserve *variety*—particularly for the season usually limited to apples and endless weeks of cabbage. With practically no extra effort (only bigger bakings to store away), the deep freezer can become a second pair of hands by preserving the extras you have made for it.

After deciding what you'd like to have on hand out of its growing season, the next decision is—how much? One detail of the answer, but a very vital one, is to pack the food in one-meal quantities to fit your family's needs. The full answer must be worked out to fit your crops or sources of supply, and (very important!) the family's preferences.

The storage capacity of deep freezers depends on the packing methods used. If all food is packed in identical packets which can be put into the freezer like a lot of bricks, you are making maximum use of freezer space. The chances are, however, that you will be using different types and shapes of packet. The following can only be rough indications of holding capacity, for as well as depending on the shapes of packet, they are dependent on the sizes of the freezer baskets or the arrangement of the freezer shelves.

Approximate holding capacity of 1 cubic foot of freezer space
16–20 identical, tub-shaped, 1-pint cartons—or
20 lb. meat or poultry—or
35–40 identical, square, or rectangular, 1-pint cartons.
When considering what to freeze, keep these points in mind:

1. *Freeze only the best when it is at its best.*
2. *Pack in one-meal quantities.*
3. *Don't put food into the freezer without having a good idea of when you mean to take it out.*
4. *Don't keep food in the freezer any longer than necessary, and certainly no longer than the recommended storage period.*
5. *Food does not improve in frozen storage.*

HOW LONG SHOULD FOOD BE DEEP FROZEN?

Don't be misguided enough to imagine that success in deep freezing is measured in terms of years. Food can be kept only for comparatively short periods (which vary with the type of food) in an *appetizing* condition. Zero temperature does not *stop* the chemical changes which spoil food—it merely slows their action. After the period of satisfactory storage of a particular food has expired— this period is called storage "life" (*see* p. 88)—it will begin to lose flavour, quality and edibility. But if the food is in perfect condition, correctly prepared, wrapped and sealed and kept in the frozen state, it will keep perfectly for the given time.

Admittedly, there is a point beyond the period of storage "life" that may still be on the right side of danger, but don't try to find it: that is probably the point when all deep-frozen food, no matter what, begins to taste the same. Those who keep well within the recommended storage periods will get most pleasure and satisfaction from their frozen foods.

To put it in a different way, it's only economic common-sense to keep food in the deep freezer for the shortest time necessary. A rapid turnover of food reduces the cost per pound of storage.

The Basic Rules

Like every process, deep freezing has its basic rules. It doesn't pay to disregard them; for although the food may keep, it will lose quality.

These are general rules. Supplementary rules, applicable only to certain foods, are listed under their respective chapter headings.

1. *Freeze only top-quality products.* Freezing cannot improve food, and freezer space is valuable. It is a waste to put in food of poor quality.

2. *Freeze food when it is at the peak of its quality*—that is, when it is ripe and ready for eating in the normal way, and preferably early in its season. Overripe fruits and vegetables are too starchy or mushy. Unripe fruit may become bitter.

3. *Handle food destined for the freezer quickly.* All food begins to deteriorate the moment it is killed or harvested. Fruits and vegetables should be frozen within six hours of picking. This can be achieved by handling small quantities at a time.

4. *Observe the basic rules of hygiene.* The food you put into the freezer must be clean.

5. *Follow the general and specific directions* and make a note of what you have done. You may find that in future you need to adapt the directions to suit the varieties of fruit and vegetables you grow.

6. *Only use packaging materials which are guaranteed to be sufficiently moisture-vapour-proof and resistant to cross-*

contamination during storage at $-5°F$. Any old packaging material *may* work, but the chances are it won't.

7. *Pack food in usable quantities.* Packing in quantities larger than those likely to be cooked and eaten at one meal leads to waste. It is unwise to re-freeze remainders.

8. *As much air as possible must be extracted from each packet and then it must be carefully and completely sealed.* The packaging material, the method of packing, and the seal are trying to protect the food from air, dehydration and cross-contamination.

9. *Label and date packets.* It is a nuisance when, opening a package you imagined to be strawberries, fish is revealed. Only by dating can you hope to arrange a sensible turnover of food in the deep freezer.

10. *Cool food to room temperature or below before putting it in the freezer.* Food packets should be frozen quickly and, for the sake of food already stored, the deep-freeze temperature should not be raised by adding too many fresh packets at a time.

11. *Limit additions of food to the freezer to the quantity advised by the manufacturer of your freezer.*

12. *Allow air spaces between packets added to the deep freezer for fast freezing.* When new packets are fully frozen, they may be tightly stacked. Follow some general system of storage, such as keeping all similar foods together.

13. *Observe suggested time limits for storage.* After a certain period of frozen storage—the period varies with the type of food—frozen food begins to lose flavour.

14. *Keep records.* Only by keeping a note of what remains in the freezer can you hope to remove food while it is

at its best. This also guards against eating all the favourite foods first, and against forgotten hoards.

15. *Plan freezing and menus so that all frozen foods are eaten by the time they are in season again.*

16. *Do not let the freezer temperature rise above 0°F and the cabinet should normally be set to run at −5°F.*

17. Never re-freeze frozen foods which have thawed.

Packaging

All food must be packed carefully, and the package sealed, before it is put into the deep freezer. Much of the success of deep-frozen storage depends on making a suitable choice of package (carton, bag, sheet or rigid container), and being sure to use packaging material that is easy to handle, and will not split, burst, leak, smell or allow odours or water vapour to escape or to invade, *while being stored at* $-5°F$.

There is a great deal of packaging material which *looks* as if it might be suitable, but unless the manufacturer or retailer will guarantee that it will stand up to zero temperature for 12 months, its use should be limited to very small experiments.

If you decide to experiment, don't forget that the result may be an unpleasant mess inside the freezer, and cross-contamination which may involve considerable quantities of food. On the whole it is probably cheaper to let the manufacturers and retailers do the experiments and wait for them to show, by labelling, when they have a satisfactory product on the market.

WHY FOOD MUST BE WRAPPED

There are a number of hazards which food in frozen storage, food prepared for storage, and food being thawed after storage, must negotiate. They are dehydration during frozen storage; oxidation reactions; and contamination by dirt, insects, moulds and crossflavours at various stages.

Low temperature storage gradually dehydrates food, and it is the function of the packaging material to resist

24

this process by minimizing the exchange of moisture in the food for air inside the deep freezer. If it fails to do this, the food will dehydrate and in doing so will suffer from the effects of oxidation. The presence of air will speed up the tendency of fats to become rancid during storage, and oxidation (visible on meat and poultry as greyish spots, and sometimes called "freezer burn") will take place.

Ordinary kitchen packing papers (lightweight foils, greaseproof and transparent papers) are not constructed for the task of protecting food in deep-freezer conditions. They may be waterproof to some extent, but most of them will allow water *vapour* to enter or escape.

For success, all packaging material used on food which is to be deep frozen must be *moisture-vapour-proof*.

CHOICE OF PACKAGING MATERIALS

Materials should be:

1. Moisture-vapour-proof.
2. Waterproof to prevent leakage, both of liquid and smells.
3. Greaseproof.
4. Odourless. (This applies also to sealing tape.)
5. Strong enough and durable.
6. Easy to handle.
7. Economical in storage space.
8. Capable of standing up to storage at $-5°F$.

PACKAGING MATERIALS

Rigid Containers. As a single purchase, the *moisture-vapour-proof plastic-box container* which is constructed to stand up to zero temperature, is the most expensive form of deep-freeze packaging material. On the other hand, once bought it can be used indefinitely, in conjunction with a zero-temperature sealing tape, and it is very economical in storage space. Such containers are particularly suitable for foods which can fill them sufficiently to eliminate pockets of air, that is, for small fruits packed in dry sugar, fruit packed in syrup, peas, mince, ice-cream, soups and purées.

Flat Waxed Carton Boxes with Lids. Used in conjunction with zero-temperature sealing tape, but without a liner, these have approximately the same uses as the rigid plastic-box container, but whether waxed cartons can be used more than once depends entirely on extremely careful cleaning, and conditions of storage between use. In general, re-use is inadvisable.

Upright Waxed Cartons. Sealed with sealing tape these can be used for purées, soups, small fruit and fruit juices.

Waxed Cartons with Liners. Can be used for vegetables, sliced meat, chops, fish and fruit. Only the liner need be sealed; the carton acts as a protector, or overwrap.

Waxed Tubs. Round, waxed tubs are less economical in storage space than square or rectangular containers, but those with lids that are guaranteed air-tight require no sealing. They are suitable for fruit in syrup and other moist or semi-moist foods such as sauces, soups and ice-cream.

Bags. Bags made of moisture-vapour-proof material capable of withstanding $-5°F$ temperature during 12 months' storage are a popular and effective type of packing for the deep freezer. A variety of sizes and shapes makes them adaptable to many types of food, such as vegetables, fish, fruits packed in sugar, and joints of regular shape. *Air pockets must be squeezed out of the bags before they are sealed.* Bags may be sealed by a fastener (*see* p. 31).

The disadvantage of bag packing is that the bag may tear, and is often unsuitable for re-use. The danger of damage to bags in the deep freezer, either from the angular nature of its contents or from frequent handling, may be considerably lessened by overwrapping. Correctly sealed bags may be overwrapped for protection in brown paper, greaseproof paper, mutton cloth or old (washed) nylon stockings. Paper bags, with moisture-vapour-proof linings (in effect, a bag equal to the conditions of zero temperature storage with an overwrap) may be bought.

Sheet Wrappings. Various types of suitable sheet wrapping can be bought and *when properly applied*, this form of wrapping, though not the least troublesome, is an effective method of eliminating air pockets from packages prior to sealing. Sheet wrappings can be well adapted for packing joints, poultry and fish, but they must be sealed with a suitable sealing tape and given some protective covering.

Examples of suitable sheet and bag materials are:

> *Visqueen Polythene film*
>
> *BX Polythene film*
>
> *Pliofilm* (*grade FM-1-80*)
>
> *Saran Wrap*

Wrapping Sealers. All packages for the deep freezer, except containers with a *guaranteed* air-tight seal equal to conditions of zero storage, must be sealed. Some materials are sealed by tape and some by covered wire fasteners.

A "bunched" bag-seal may be made by the correct application of a covered wire fastener (*see* p. 32).

Rigid containers, cartons and boxes should be sealed with a special sealing tape which is odourless and equal to the conditions of −5°F storage. Tape made from any of the materials listed under Sheet Wrappings would be suitable.

PACKAGING MATERIALS TO BE AVOIDED

1. Any material which is not guaranteed moisture-vapour-proof and equal to 12 months' storage at −5°F.
2. Materials which leak.
3. Materials which rust.
4. Materials which may break or become brittle during −5°F storage. Glass and plastics *which have not been designed* for storage at −5°F both fall within this group.

Before buying any packaging materials for the deep freezer, always ask:

Are they moisture-vapour-proof?
Will they stand up to 12 months' storage at −5°F?
Are they odourless in themselves?

HOW TO PACK

Good packing and good packaging materials must go together, for one without the other is quite useless. If packing technique is poor and allows air to get into the food through an ineffective seal, the result will be, if not repellent, disappointing and displeasing.

The technique of packing is first of all to eliminate air from the package, and then by good sealing, to *keep* it out.

If air is allowed to remain in a package, desiccation of the food will take place and there can be a change in the composition of food juices. If you find a heavy deposit of frost on the inner surface of a package taken from the deep freezer, you will know that you haven't been successful in eliminating air pockets from the package *before* you sealed it.

Packing in Sheet Materials. Place food to be wrapped in the centre of the sheet. Draw two sides of sheet together above the food and fold them over and over downwards, towards the food, to make a wrapping that is as tight and close to the food as possible. Fold the ends like a parcel, being sure to get them as close and tight to the food as you can, pressing out all air pockets. All folds must be sealed with a deep-freeze sealing tape.

It is as well to "overwrap" parcel packs of angular food in greaseproof or brown paper, mutton cloth or old nylon stockings. The overwrap will not need an air-tight fastening.

Packing in Bags. See that the bags are completely opened before filling.

When filling bags with a *liquid or semi-liquid* food see that this fills the corners of the bags and that no air pockets are left. It is better to use some sort of funnel for this type of food so that the top of the bag (the sealing edges) remain dry.

When filling with solid food, pack this neatly into the bag, then press out air pockets as carefully as you can.

Headspaces. Liquid and semi-liquid food will expand while it is freezing, so room must be allowed for this between the food and the seal of the package. If this is not done, the contents will expand and may break the containers.

General directions for headspaces are that approximately ½-inch headspace should be left between *most* foods and the seals of their containers: ½–1-inch headspace should be left between liquids and the container seal.

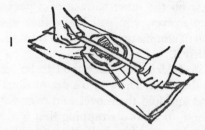

Tape-sealed sheet wrapping. Lay joint on sheet. Fold two sides over meat and tape-seal down centre (1). Fold unsealed ends across package (2). Seal both ends separately, after pressing out air (3). Slip package into length of mutton cloth or clean nylon stocking (4).

Waxed cartons, unless guaranteed air-tight, must be tape-sealed (5).

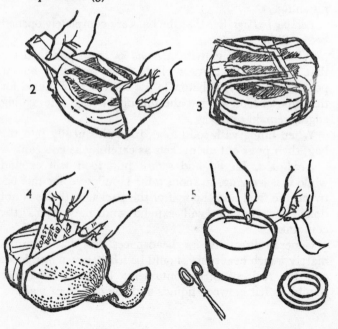

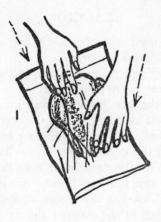

Bunched bag-seal. Extract air from bag by careful pressing (1). Twist the plastic-covered fastener round the neck of bag (2), turn the top of the bag down over this first twist, seal by twice re-crossing fastener round the "bunch".

SEALING

Successful sealing is essential if you are to get the best results from your deep freezer.

The bunched bag seal. A simple, inexpensive seal for bag packs is the covered wire tie-fastener.

First see that the food is packed well into the bag and that no air pockets have been left in the corners. Press out obvious air pockets. Continue squeezing bag towards its mouth bunching the unfilled part of the bag together in the left hand. With the right hand twist the neck of the bag and wind the fastener tightly round once only. Bring the top of the bag down *over* the crossed fastener, and cross the ends of the fastener tightly over this and then re-cross them. Complete the seal by twisting the ends of the fastener neatly.

Sealing Lined Cartons. Heat-sealing linings of cartons can be sealed in the same way as heat-sealing bags. When filling, make sure that the lining is fully open and pressed into the corners of the carton. Headspace should be left when necessary. It is necessary to seal the outer carton.

Sealing Unlined Cartons and Tubs and Rigid Containers. Unless these have a lid which is *guaranteed* air-tight, these must be sealed with a deep-freeze sealing tape.

Make sure no air pockets have been left in the carton, and that sufficient headspace has been allowed for expansion. Put on lid and seal the edges completely with a continuous length of sealing tape, making sure to leave no wrinkles or folds in the tape.

LABELLING

All packets should be completely labelled and dated before they are put into the freezer. If you cannot write on the packet, stick on a label indicating the contents and the date of freezing, and cover it with a piece of sealing tape to keep it in place. Ink smudges in the freezer and it is recommended to use pencil or waxed pencil (chinagraph) on labels. Always use a chinagraph or "felt" pencil when writing labels as ordinary lead will fade after a period of low temperature storage. The pencils can be bought at any good stationers.

Don't forget that good packing with suitable materials can extend the storage "life" of foods, but neither can offset faulty preparation, or make poor-quality food better. High-quality food, correct and speedy preparation, proper storage, and good packing are all essential. None of them should be neglected.

PUTTING FOOD IN THE DEEP FREEZER

Additions of food to the freezer should be limited to the quantity advised by the manufacturer of your freezer. They should be frozen as quickly as possible, to avoid raising the temperature in the freezer.

If the freezer has a separate freezing compartment, put new additions in this, and remove and pack closely in the general storage space when fully frozen. Air spaces should be allowed between packets of food while being frozen.

Quickest freezing is achieved by making sure that all new packets are in contact with a refrigerated surface. There is a danger, when this isn't possible or when additions of food are packed into the freezer too closely, that those in the middle may not freeze rapidly enough. Foods should reach $-5°F$ in 24 hours. This may not be achieved if, in bulk, additions to the freezer exceed one fifteenth (or at most one-tenth) of the total capacity of your freezer. When food is frozen too slowly, spoilage may result.

KEEPING RECORDS

All plans concerning what to freeze and when to use the food may go awry if they are not supported by some form of record system. The facts one has to know, *not guess*, are:

1. *Where was the food put?*
2. *How much has been used?*
3. *When must it all be taken out?*

One very simple method is to "catalogue", in an indexed loose-leaf book, or on a piece of slate. Only essential details need be recorded, for example:

					No:	Use before:
Basket or Shelf	A.	Pheasant	3̸ 2̸ 1			13/6/60
			3̸, 2̸, 1 to indicate 1 pheasant is left.			
,,	,,	,,	B. Trout	4̸ 3̸ 2 1		9/9/60
,,	,,	,,	C. Raspberries	2̸ 1		6/8/60

Meat

All meat deep freezes well, and sometimes tender meat becomes a little tenderer in storage. But do not think the deep freezer is a tenderizer that will make tough meat more edible. It won't, nor can it add more flavour. It is more practical to try and soften tough meat in a stew than to waste freezer space on it.

Every inch of freezer space is valuable and costs some money. Make the most of it by only freezing tender meat of highest quality.

Many butchers are getting accustomed to the idea of their customers buying meat for deep freezing and will, by arrangement, cut into suitable joints or the meat can be bought at wholesale prices and you can ask your own butcher to cut it up for you but remember that he has to live as well as you and don't expect him to do it for nothing.

BASIC RULES

1. Good quality is essential whether you are choosing a live animal for slaughter or buying from the butcher.
2. Carcases should be quickly and thoroughly chilled after slaughter.
3. Veal and pork should be packed and put in the freezer within 24–48 hours of slaughtering. Beef and lamb should be packed and put in the freezer within 7–10 days of slaughtering.
4. Do not store more meat than can be used within the recommended storage period.

5. Do not prepare more meat than the freezer can take at one time. If packing more, hold additional unfrozen food in a refrigerator, or under a fan, or in a very cold larder, and put into the freezer later.
6. Bone meat when possible. Bones take up space and are apt to tear the wrapping material.
7. Trim off surplus fat.
8. Always use moisture-vapour-proof wrapping materials.
9 Be sure to exclude all possible air before sealing packages.
10. Freeze immediately.
11. Keep records.

PACKING

Meat should be prepared for the deep freezer as soon as it is cut. It is particularly important to trim off surplus fat both to save space and guard against rancidity which becomes apparent more quickly in fat than in lean meat. Pork fat is particularly susceptible to rancidity; and this is accentuated if there is too great a delay between slaughter and freezing.

Whether packing joints, chops or steaks, try to make the meat compact so that air can more readily be excluded during packing.

In general, moisture-vapour-proof paper in combination with the parcel pack, is the most satisfactory method of packing meat. Projecting bones may be padded with greaseproof paper or clean rag before wrapping. If doubtful about the strength of the moisture-vapour-proof paper, overwrap the package with greaseproof paper, brown paper or a stocking.

CHOPS AND STEAKS

Before packing chops and steaks, consider how many are likely to be needed for each meal and apportion quantities accordingly.

Place a fold of transparent or greaseproof paper between chops or steaks before packing so that they can be separated when removed from the freezer for cooking. Press the pack tightly together to exclude air. Pack compactly in moisture-vapour-proof paper or containers and seal.

MINCE

Trim off as much fat as possible before putting meat through the mincer. Pack mince tightly into a moisture-vapour-proof bag or carton, excluding air pockets and seal.

Mince balls may be made—though it would be more economical to sacrifice the traditional shape and make them into squares—and packed in usable quantities. Strictly limit the amount of seasoning, or omit it altogether and add when eaten. The addition of salt will reduce the period of satisfactory storage.

MEAT FOR STEWS

Stewing steak may be trimmed of fat, cut into cubes and pressed firmly down into a moisture-vapour-proof container.

OFFAL

It is very important that offal for the freezer should be fresh, and that it should be packaged and frozen quickly.

Liver and heart may be frozen whole or sliced. If sliced, separate the slices with two pieces of transparent or greaseproof paper before overall wrapping.

Tongue, heart and kidneys should not be stored for longer than 3–4 months. Liver should not be stored for longer than 2–3 months.

SAUSAGES

Limit the amount of seasoning while making sausages, because all seasonings tend to become stronger in deep-frozen food. Salt speeds up rancidity in frozen fat, so make sausages that are to be frozen without salt, and remember to add it during cooking. Unsalted, unseasoned sausage meat will store satisfactorily for 6 months. Salted, seasoned sausages should not be kept for longer than 1 month.

HAMS AND BACON

There is no point in deep-freezing hams and bacon because they keep better in cold storage ($32° - 34°F$) than in $-5°F$ storage. In addition, the freezer "life" of hams and bacon in the piece is limited to 3–4 months. Sliced bacon may be kept in the deep freezer for convenience, wrapped and sealed, but its freezer 'life" is little more than 3 weeks.

If, however, you have killed a pig it is perfectly satisfactory to keep one of the hams in your deep freeze, after brining it, particularly if your larder storage conditions are not very satisfactory. The ham should be particularly well wrapped in two bags one inside the other before freezing.

BULK BUYING OF MEAT

If you are in a position to get meat at reduced price for quantity of if you have your own meat, beef, lamb or pork, available for deep freezing you must remember that it will use up a large amount of space in your cabinet, and can sometimes be almost an embarrassment unless you have a large family. For myself I feel that a quarter of beef is really too much for most people, and it might be a better proposition to ask your wholesaler to select some special joints such as topside, rolled ribs, and so on, and then get these cut into the size you are likely to want. A lamb of course is a different matter and can be dealt with in the usual joints, leg, shoulder, loin, etc., the head not being worth freezing or the neck end which takes up too much space. Half a pig is a good buy, and provided it is not too fat it freezes well.

Beef and lamb have the longest freezer life,

	8–9 months.
Veal and pork	5–6 months.

COOKING FROZEN MEAT

To get the best results from frozen meat it is essential to use the "slow" roasting method, that is 20–25 minutes per pound of meat at 300°–350°F or Mark 3–4. If you are using an Aga then roast with the lid open or put a pan of water in the oven before starting to cook.

Meat CAN be cooked straight from the freezer without pre-thawing but this should only be done in an emergency. If you have to do so then you can take as a guide the fact that completely frozen joints take from 1½ times to twice as long to cook as thawed out joints, for example

5 lb. of beef thawed out needs 25 minutes per pound,

2 hours and 5 minutes.

Same joint still frozen   3½–4 hours.

NB. Once thawed out, meat must never be re-frozen.

Fish

Only really fresh fish should be frozen, and the freezer "life" of fish is comparatively short. Recommended storage periods for the fatty fish—salmon, halibut, herring, mackerel, turbot, eels, for instance—are as low as 2 months. Those for the lean fish, such as cod, flounder, plaice, sole, trout and whiting, are about 4 months.

It is, however, a great advantage to have a little fish in the deep freezer to provide variety on the menu, and a tremendous advantage to be able to store part of a salmon for most people quickly tire of eating this rich fish.

METHOD

1. Fish should be killed at once and put on ice until it can be prepared for the deep freezer. Freeze within 24 hours of being caught.
2. Scale, if necessary, and remove fins.
3. Gut.
4. Small fish, such as trout, may be left whole. Large fish should have their heads and tails removed, and be packed either whole or in steaks. Flat fish may be skinned and filleted.
5. Dip whole lean fish, steaks or fillets into cold salted water (1 tablespoonful salt per quart of water), and drain. Fat fish—whole, steaks or fillets—should be wiped over with fresh water.
6. Pack in moisture-vapour-proof paper, carton or bag, seal and freeze. Several fillets or steaks may be packed together to suit family needs, each piece

separated from the other by two sheets of transparent paper, and then packed together into an overall container, and sealed.

THAWING AND COOKING

Fish intended for a *slow* method of cooking may be cooked frozen or thawed. If cooked frozen, extra cooking time must be allowed. Fish intended for *rapid* cooking—such as frying—should be thawed before cooking, and it is advisable to partially thaw thick, round fish before cooking by any method, owing to the difficulty of judging heat penetration.

Thaw all fish slowly in a cool place in unopened packages.

CRAB

Start with a live crab and kill it either by driving a skewer into the brain or dropping it into boiling water—whichever method seems the least unkind. Cook by bringing slowly to the boil in salted water, allowing 15 minutes to the pound.

Drain and cool the cooked crab thoroughly.

Open the crab and take out any green matter, the small sac in the top of the big shell, the lungs and "fingers", and throw all these away.

Take the edible meat from the claws and body, and pack it into moisture-vapour-proof bags or cartons, leaving ½-inch headspace. Seal and freeze.

Crabs should not be stored for longer than 1 month.

Thaw in its container and serve while it is still very cold.

LOBSTER

Start with a live lobster and kill it according to the method of your choice (*see* Crab). Simmer in boiling

salted water, allowing 10–15 minutes to the pound. Cool
and split. Remove the intestine (the black line which runs
down through the tail) and the sac in the head.

Remove meat from shell and pack into moisture-vapour-
proof bags or cartons, leaving ½-inch headspace. Seal and
freeze.

Lobster should not be stored for more than 1 month.

OYSTERS

Wash the oysters to remove dirt, then remove from the
shells. It is important not to lose the oyster "juice"; save
this on one side.

Wash the oysters in cold salted water (2 tablespoonfuls
salt per quart of water) and drain. Pack in watertight
containers, adding the saved "juice". Leave ½-inch headspace. Seal and freeze.

Thawed oysters may be eaten raw, or cooked. Store for
not more than 1 month.

PRAWNS AND SHRIMPS

Boil prawns or shrimps in salted water for 3–5 minutes,
depending on size, Cool them in the water, and then shell.
If the prawns are large enough to have a visible vein
along the back, it should be removed. Cool thoroughly
and pack into moisture-vapour-proof bags, leaving ½-inch
headspace. Seal and freeze.

Potted shrimps may also be packed in cartons for the
deep freezer, but it is important to use less seasoning than
for usual potting.

Prawns and shrimps should not be stored for longer
than 1 month.

Poultry

All kinds of poultry may be frozen, and if the varieties put into the freezer are at the right stage of development, correctly killed, well-packed and removed before the suggested storage limit has expired, this is one of the most successful frozen foods.

One of the greatest advantages of the deep freezer is that it enables its owner to buy poultry when prices are low, or to kill surplus poultry, and store for future use.

METHOD

1. Starve the bird for 24 hours before killing.
2. Hang and bleed well after slaughter.
3. *Pluck and remove all quills.* If scalded, avoid over-scalding, for this increases the chances of freezer-burn (grey spots which appear during storage and are more usually caused by incorrect wrapping). It is advisable to keep the scald between 125° and 135°F. Avoid any damage to the skin.
4. Put the bird into a refrigerator or a cool larder for 12 hours, or overnight.
5. Remove head, feet, oil sac and draw, putting the giblets on one side.
6. If necessary, wash and drain.

PREPARING WHOLE BIRDS

Truss the bird and tie it as for cooking. Whole birds may be stuffed before freezing, but this will limit the safe freezing period to the storage limit of the stuffing (*see*

43

Storage Chart, p. 88). It is essential that stuffing should be cold before being put into the cavity.

Wrap the bird in a strong moisture-vapour-proof material or put in a moisture-vapour-proof bag, being careful to exclude as much air as possible from the package. If there are any sharp bones, these may first be covered with small pieces of transparent or greaseproof paper, so that they do not pierce the overall wrapping. Seal and freeze.

JOINTED BIRDS

Poultry may be frozen in joints or pieces. Broilers may be split in two along the back and breastbone, fryers and fowl cut into sizes suited to one's needs. It is often convenient to separate the choice pieces (such as breasts) or meaty pieces (such as thighs) from the bony legs, wings and backs. This may be done for separate packing and freezing; or the bony pieces may be eaten fresh or boned for use in pre-cooked dishes, and then stored in the freezer.

All joints, or pieces of poultry should be washed, drained and cooled, prior to packaging.

Halves of Poultry should be placed together with two pieces of wrapping material between them before overall wrapping.

Breasts or Bony Pieces of poultry may be placed in separate folds of paper—with air pockets excluded—and then packed into a moisture-vapour-proof container, or wrapped in moisture-vapour-proof paper and sealed.

Giblets are best when fresh. When frozen they have a much shorter satisfactory storage life than poultry.

44

Prepare giblets for the freezer by cleaning, washing, drying and chilling before wrapping. Wrap in moisture-vapour-proof paper or bag, excluding air pockets. Always pack and freeze giblets separately, unless poultry packed with giblets is to be removed from the freezer within the recommended storage period of giblets. When this is planned, the giblets may be wrapped and placed in the cavity of the bird. Chicken livers are worth freezing separately; as they are useful for making several tasty dishes.

Stuffings. As all seasoning tends to become stronger during frozen storage, it is advisable to limit it to less than would be used in stuffings for immediate use. Pork sausage meat should not be used if the stuffing is to be placed in the cavity of the bird. The best stuffing for this means of packing is a lightly-seasoned bread-crumb stuffing.

Unless a stuffed bird is being prepared for some special, future event (within the storage period of the stuffing), it is advisable to pack and freeze the stuffing separately. Pack in a moisture-vapour-proof paper or bag, seal and freeze.

THAWING AND COOKING THE FROZEN BIRD

Ideally, poultry should be thawed in a refrigerator. Thawing times will depend to a large extent on the size of the bird. A 4-lb. bird will take 12-16 hours to thaw in a refrigerator, a large roaster or boiling fowl up to 24 hours. Remove the packaging and leave the bird on a plate in the refrigerator until it is pliable.

To thaw more quickly, the bird may be left in a cool place where the temperature does not exceed 60–65°F.

This method takes about half the time of thawing in the refrigerator.

QUICK COOKING

Joints of poultry to be deep-fried or cooked by any quick cooking method should be thawed beforehand.

Game

Ideally, all game birds should be prepared for the deep freezer in the same way as domestic poultry, but this is seldom possible and often would not suit individual tastes.

The poulterer of course always freezes his game with fur and feathers on as, if he has to sell if after deep freezing, this is the only state in which he can do so. It is quite satisfactory from the keeping point of view, but plucking, skinning and eviscerating after thawing has been done is an unpleasant task at the best, and unless you have urgent reason for freezing this way we do not advise it.

METHOD

1. Bleed the bird as soon as it is shot.
2. Keep it in the coolest place available until you get it home.
3. Hang until it is sufficiently gamey for your taste.
4. Pluck.
5. Remove as much shot as possible.
6. Draw.
7. Wash and drain cavity.
8. Wipe over body with a damp cloth.
9. Pack.
10. Cool.
11. Freeze.

It is advisable to draw any water fowl which may have been feeding on fish as soon as possible after shooting so that the fishy flavour does not extend to the flesh, but this, of course, will limit the period of hanging.

Game birds are packed for the freezer and prepared for cooking in the same way as poultry.

HARES AND RABBITS

1. Behead and bleed hares and rabbits as soon as possible after killing.
2. Hang for up to 24 hours in a cool temperature.
3. Skin and eviscerate.
4. Wash and drain cavity.
5. Wipe the carcase over with a damp cloth.
6. Cut into joints.
7. Each joint should be placed in a separate fold of paper, being careful to exclude air pockets, and then packed together into a moisture-vapour-proof container, or wrapped in moisture-vapour-proof paper and sealed.

VENISON

Anyone who is not used to large-scale jointing will find venison difficult to prepare. If a butcher is available, give him the carcase to prepare and joint, then pack the joints you wish to freeze in the same way as you would pack joints of meat. Those who cannot, or who do not wish to call in aid, should follow these directions:

1. Behead and bleed the venison.
2. Skin.
3. Eviscerate.
4. Remove shot.
5. Wash the interior with cold water.
6. Wipe exterior with a cloth which has been wrung out in cold water.

7. Prop open the belly with a stick so that air may get to it.
8. Hang in the coolest place available—ideally the temperature should be just above freezing point—for 24 hours—or until it has reached the desired condition, protecting from flies, vermin, etc.
9. Cut into joints, cutting away the flesh about the wound.
10. Pack as for joints of meat.
11. Freeze.

All game must be hung *before* freezing. If hanging after freezing and thawing is attempted, the flesh will just go bad.

Vegetables

Pick vegetables for the deep freezer when they are young and tender. It is a waste of time and space to wait until they've got to horticultural show proportions before you freeze them.

Most vegetables freeze well. The *exceptions* are raw onions, radishes, raw celery, cucumbers, lettuce and similar salad vegetables. These should *not* be frozen.

METHOD

1. Pick young vegetables, preferably early in the morning.
2. Wash thoroughly in cold water.
3. Cut or sort into similar sizes, rejecting all imperfect vegetables.
4. Blanch.
5. Cool in iced or running water.
6. Drain.
7. Pack and seal.
8. Freeze.

TO BLANCH IN BOILING WATER

All vegetables, except green peppers and parsley, *must* be blanched in boiling water or steam to retard the action of enzymes (chemical agents within the plants) which, if allowed to remain fully active, would quickly lower the quality and flavour of the vegetables during storage.

Blanch only 1 lb. of vegetables at a time to make sure of thorough blanching, and to prevent any quick change in the temperature of the water. Three to four quarts of boiling water per pound of vegetables should be allowed.

Put the washed, cut or assorted vegetables into a wire basket or cheese-cloth bag and completely immerse in a saucepan of fast boiling water. Cover with a tight lid. Blanching time varies with each vegetable (*see* specific directions, pp. 53–59), and should be counted from the moment the water comes to the boil again. If the water takes more than 1 minute to re-boil, smaller quantities of vegetables should be used unless boiling can be speeded up by increased heat under the saucepan.

Bring water back to fast boiling point before immersing another basketful of vegetables.

TO BLANCH IN STEAM

Put sufficient water in the saucepan below the steamer to prevent it boiling dry.

When water is boiling fast, place 1 lb. vegetables in the wire basket or cheese-cloth bag and lower it into the steamer. Cover with lid.

Begin to count blanching time (*see* specific directions, pp. 53–59) from the moment steam begins to escape from the lid. *In general, steam-blanching takes half as long again as blanching in boiling water.* If blanching directions indicate 2 minutes in boiling water, steam-blanch for 3 minutes.

Steam-blanching is not recommended for leafy green vegetables such as spinach. In steam, the leaves tend to mat together.

COOLING

When blanching time is up, remove the vegetables from the boiling water or steam and immerse the wire basket or cheese-cloth bag in cold running water, adding ice-cubes if available. Vegetables which are not quickly cooled become mushy. Leave the vegetables in cold water only long enough to cool them through to the centre. Before being packed for the freezer they should be cooled to 60°F or lower. A general rule is to cool for the time equal to blanching time in a large quantity of water. Drain thoroughly.

PACKING

Observe the general rules of packing, choosing packet sizes that will suit your family or your dinner-party needs.

BRINE PACKING

Whether to pack dry or pack in brine is very controversial. Some authorities incline to think that vegetables wet-packed in brine are less subject to toughening during storage. On the other hand, brine packing is more troublesome.

Most of the non-leafy vegetables (e.g. asparagus, runner beans, broccoli, brussels sprouts, cauliflower, peas) may be wet-packed in brine.

Prepare according to the general rules (p. 50) and specific directions (pp. 53–59). When vegetables have been blanched, cooled and drained, pack them into rigid containers to within $\frac{1}{2}$–1 inch of the top and then just cover with 2% cold brine solution (2 tablespoonfuls salt per quart of water). Rigid containers are better for all wet packs. Leave headspace, seal and freeze.

FREEZING

Freeze vegetables immediately after packing. If delay in doing this is unavoidable, keep the packets in the refrigerator or the coolest place available until they can be put in the freezer.

DIRECTIONS FOR INDIVIDUAL VEGETABLES

When time for only one blanching method is given, that is considered the better method.

All vegetables must be cooled and drained before packing.

All vegetable packets must be sealed.

ASPARAGUS

Choose young, fat stalks. Avoid those that are thin and woody. Trim off inedible part of stalk and arrange spears in equal lengths.

	Boiling Water	*Steam*
Small	2 min.	3 min.
Medium	3 min.	4½ min.
Thick	4 min.	6 min.

BEANS, Broad

Choose broad beans that are small and young. Do not wait until the outer skin is leathery. Shell.

Boiling Water	*Steam*
3 min.	4½ min.

Pack in bags or cartons, leaving ½-inch headspace.

BEANS, Runner and French

Choose young, tender, stringless beans. Cut off ends and tips. If very small, leave whole, otherwise cut into 1-inch lengths, or slice.

	Boiling Water	*Steam*
Whole beans	2–3 min.	3–4 min.
Cut beans	2 min.	3 min.
Sliced beans	1 min.	2 min.

Pack in bags or cartons, leaving ½-inch headspace.

BEETROOT

Choose young beetroots, not more than 3 inches in diameter. Trim, then cook in boiling water until tender (25–50 minutes) taking care not to bleed them. Cool in cold water and skin. Slice or dice. Pack in bags or cartons leaving ½-inch headspace.

BROCCOLI

Choose compact heads with tender stalks. Discard any woody pieces, and cut to size.

	Boiling Water	Steam
Thin stalks	3 min.	4 min.
Medium stalks	4 min.	5 min.
Thick stalks	5 min.	6 min.

When packing, arrange tips in opposite directions. No headspace is necessary.

BRUSSELS SPROUTS

Choose small, tight heads. Trim and grade for size.

	Boiling Water
Small sprouts	3 min.
Medium sprouts	4 min.

No headspace is needed in packing.

CABBAGE

(Do not take freezing space for this if more interesting vegetables are likely to be available.)

Trim and shred the head of a young crisp cabbage. Blanch for 1½ minutes in boiling water. Frozen cabbage should not be used, uncooked, in salads. Pack, leaving ½-inch headspace.

CARROTS

Choose young, or not larger than medium-sized carrots. Wash thoroughly and scale before rubbing off skin.

	Boiling Water
Whole carrots	5 min.

Pack whole, if small, or sliced or diced.

Sliced or diced carrots require ½-inch headspace in package.

CAULIFLOWER

Choose firm, compact heads. Trim, and break or cut into small pieces not larger than 1-inch across.

Boiling Water	Steam
3 min.	5 min.

No headspace is needed in packing.

CORN

On-the-Cob. The corn must be tender and fresh. Remove husk and silk, and grade for size.

	Boiling Water
Small cobs	4 min.
Medium cobs	6 min.
Large cobs	8 min.

No headspace is needed in packing.

Whole-kernel. Remove husk and silk. Wash. Cook cobs in boiling water for 4 minutes. Cool in cold water and drain. Cut kernels off cob, pack into containers, leaving ½-inch headspace.

55

KOHLRABI

Choose only young and tender kohlrabi. Trim, wash and peel. Very small kohlrabi may be left whole—others should be diced.

	Boiling Water	Steam
Whole kohlrabi	3 min.	4½ min.
Diced	2 min.	3 min.

If diced leave ½-inch headspace.

MARROW

If you wish to freeze very young marrow (the size that can be eaten whole, including skin and seed) cut into ½-inch slices, or in half if they are small enough, blanch in boiling water for 3 minutes. Larger marrows should be peeled, the seeds removed, cooked until soft, and finally mashed. Both types will require ½-inch headspace.

MIXED VEGETABLES

Prepare each vegetable according to individual directions, and combine after each has been blanched and cooled. Pack, leaving ½-inch headspace.

MUSHROOMS

Be sure to choose mushrooms that are fresh and free from decay. Wash thoroughly and trim stems. If mushrooms are larger than 1-inch across they should be sliced. Cultivated mushrooms need not be peeled. Mushrooms may be heated in melted butter (1 lb. mushrooms to 6 tablespoonfuls of butter) for 4–5 minutes, or until almost cooked, and cooled by putting pan in which they were cooked in cold water, before being packed for the freezer (leaving ½-inch headspace), or they may be prepared in the more usual way.

Steam

Whole mushrooms up to 1-inch diameter 5 min.
Button mushrooms or quarters 3½ min.
Sliced mushrooms 3 min.
Pack, leaving ½-inch headspace.

PARSLEY

Frozen parsley can only be used in stews, etc. It is unsuitable for a garnish as it becomes limp when thawed.

Wash and cut stems. Pack in small quantities. Do not blanch, but dry carefully before packing.

PARSNIPS

Choose small, young parsnips. Trim and peel. Cut into narrow strips or dice.

Boiling Water
2 min.

Pack, leaving ½-inch headspace.

PEAS

Choose young, sweet peas. Old, starchy peas are not worth freezing. Shell.

	Boiling Water	*Steam*
Small peas	1 min.	1½ min.
Medium peas	1½ min.	2 min.

Pack, leaving ½-inch headspace.

PEPPERS

Choose firm, glossy peppers of uniform colour. Wash, remove seeds and stem. Slice or dice. Pack without leaving any headspace.

Peppers may be blanched in boiling water (2 minutes

for slices), but if this is done ½-inch headspace must be left in the package.

SPINACH

Choose young fresh spinach without heavy midribs (this rule applies to all the "greens"). Wash very thoroughly. Blanch only a small amount at a time and agitate the container during blanching to separate the leaves and ensure heat penetration.

Boiling Water
2 min.

Pack, leaving ½-inch headspace.

TURNIPS

Choose small, young turnips of a mild-flavoured variety. Trim, peel and dice.

Boiling Water	*Steam*
2½ min.	4 min.

Pack, leaving ½-inch headspace.

VEGETABLE PURÉES

These may usefully be prepared and frozen for baby foods and soups.

Cook vegetable until it is tender. Drain and cool slightly, then put through a sieve, or chop finely. Chill rapidly to 60°F maximum. The easiest method is to place purée in a basin over cold running water. Pack, leaving ½-inch headspace, seal and freeze at once.

COOKING FROZEN VEGETABLES

Frozen vegetables are like fresh vegetables, and the surest way of spoiling them is overcooking. It is, of course, particularly important to guard against this, as frozen vegetables have been partially cooked before freezing. Cook for about *half* the time fresh vegetables would take.

Boiling. Most frozen vegetables may be boiled while fully frozen. The exceptions are leafy vegetables, such as spinach, which should be partially thawed before cooking to separate the leaves and ensure even heating, and corn-on-the-cob which must be completely thawed otherwise the kernels would be cooked while the cob was still a block of ice.

Steaming. It is better to partially thaw all vegetables that are to be steamed to make sure of total steam penetration.

Baking. Thaw the vegetables until they can be separated, and drain. Put the vegetables in a greased casserole with butter and seasoning. Cover and bake in the oven; 30 minutes at 350°F should be ample time for most vegetables.

Frying. Use a heavy frying-pan that can be covered. Put 1 tablespoonful of butter in the pan. Melt but do not boil. Add 1 pint frozen vegetables and cook gently until the pieces can be separated. Cover pan and cook over moderate heat until tender.

Cooked frozen vegetables may be used in the same way as cooked fresh vegetables.

Fruit

An all-the-year-round supply of summer fruits is one of the simplest but most luxurious pleasures of deep-freezer ownership. Fruit is very easy to prepare for the freezer, and nearly all fruit gives a satisfactory deep-frozen result. Best results are obtained from the tart or full, round-flavoured fruits such as gooseberries, raspberries and strawberries. "Soft"-flavoured fruits, such as pears, do not freeze well.

Fruit needs no blanching. In general, sugar is used to retard the action of enzymes while fruit is in the freezer, though some fruits may be packed without sugar or syrup, e.g. currants, gooseberries, raspberries and rhubarb, a method which slightly shortens the period of satisfactory storage. The choice of packing method depends on the subsequent use. Fruits frozen without sugar, or frozen with dry sugar, are less liquid and therefore more useful for cooking. Fruits frozen in syrup are excellent for desserts.

METHOD

1. Choose first-quality fruit, avoiding unripe fruit which will be tasteless and dull-coloured, and over-ripe fruit which will become mushy.
2. Discard any defective fruit.
3. Wash fruit rapidly in water. Do not let it stand in water, but use a wire basket or colander. Be careful not to bruise.
4. Drain thoroughly.
5. Mash, slice or purée fruit destined to be frozen in this way.

6. Pack unsweetened, with dry sugar, or with syrup (*see* separate directions, below).
7. Seal.
8. Freeze.

UNSWEETENED PACKING

This method is only satisfactory with fruit which can be prepared without breaking the skin, or with fruit which does not discolour during preparation. Prepare according to the general directions, pack into containers and leave ½-inch headspace.

DRY SUGAR PACKING

This method is most suitable for crushed or sliced fruit, or for soft, juicy fruit whose juice draws easily.

Wash and drain fruit and prepare it as you would for the table. Put the fruit in a large bowl and sprinkle with sugar. The quantity of sugar needed varies with the tartness of the fruit, ranging from 3–5 lb. fruit to 1 lb. sugar. Mix sugar and fruit by gently shaking the bowl or stirring with a silver spoon until the sugar is dissolved. Pack into containers, leaving ½-inch headspace.

Another dry sugar packing method is to add the sugar *during* packing. Put a little fruit in the package, sprinkle with sugar. Add another layer of fruit, then a layer of sugar. Continue in this way. The correct proportions of fruit and sugar must be observed. Pack into containers, leaving ½-inch headspace.

SYRUP PACKING

Syrup packing is the best method for non-juicy fruits, and for fruits which discolour easily during preparation.

The strength of syrup depends on the sourness of the fruit and individual taste. A 40% syrup suits most tastes, but a weaker syrup should be used for very delicately flavoured fruit, otherwise the taste of sugar will predominate.

Syrup is made by dissolving sugar in hot or cold water, but it *must be cold before being added to the fruit*. Syrups may be prepared in advance and kept for a day in a cold larder or refrigerator.

Sugar	Water		Syrup
2 cups	4 cups	=	30% Light syrup
3 cups	4 cups	=	40% Medium syrup
4 cups	4 cups	=	50% Heavy syrup

Pack prepared fruit into containers and cover with syrup, leaving $\frac{1}{2}$–1-inch headspace. It is important that fruit should be kept well down in the syrup to prevent discoloration. Place a small piece of cellophane or similar material over the fruit and press it down into the syrup before sealing.

All fruit packets must be sealed.

HEADSPACE ALLOWANCES

Leave headspace for all fruit packed in sugar, syrup or juice, and for pulped or puréed fruit.

Allow $\frac{1}{2}$-inch for all dry packs.

For *narrow-topped wet packs* allow $\frac{3}{4}$-inch per pint.

For *wide-topped wet packs* allow $\frac{1}{2}$–1-inch per pint.

Double headspace allowance is needed for quart containers.

DISCOLORATION

Some fruits, such as apples and peaches, are subject to discoloration or darkening during preparation, storage and thawing. There are several ways of preventing this: you can work with small quantities of fruit at speed; you can slice fruit directly into the container which has previously been partly filled with syrup; or you can slice fruit into a weak solution of lemon juice and water (juice of 1 lemon to 1½ pints water) prior to packing.

PREVENTION OF DISCOLORATION DURING THAWING

Fruits subject to discoloration benefit by rapid thawing. Fruit which has been frozen unsweetened should be put immediately into hot syrup.

It sometimes helps to put a packet of fruit which has been frozen in sugar or syrup upside down in a bowl while thawing, to make sure that all the fruit is covered with sugar or syrup during thawing.

THAWING

All frozen fruit should be thawed in its original *unopened* container.

Fruits intended for open pies, etc., must be thawed sufficiently to allow them to be spread.

Fruits for use with sponge-cakes, etc., should be thawed just short of complete de-frosting.

Fruits to be used with ice-cream should only be partially de-frosted.

Fruits to be eaten raw should have a few ice-crystals left. They should be served as soon as they have reached this stage.

Thawing times	*In re-frigerator*	*At room temperature*	*In basin of cool water*
1 lb. fruit packed in syrup	6–9 hours	2–4 hours	½–1 hour

63

Fruit in dry sugar packets thaws rather more quickly than fruit in syrup packets. Unsweetened fruit packets take longer to thaw than syrup packs.

COOKING

Thaw fruit in original unopened container, until it can be separated, and then cook in the normal way. Water may be added if there is insufficient. Do not forget, when adding sugar, that the fruit will already be fairly sweet if it has been packed in sugar or syrup.

DIRECTIONS FOR INDIVIDUAL FRUITS

APPLES

There are so many varieties of apples that freezing directions are subject to a great deal of trial and error. It is best to make a few trial packets with the kinds you grow before packing a large quantity.

Choose firm, crisp apples. Wash, peel, core and slice.

Dry Sugar Pack. Slice apples into a solution of salt and water to prevent discoloration (1 teaspoonful salt to 2 quarts water). Do not leave in solution for more than 5 minutes. Drain. Sprinkle sugar over apple slices in the proportion of $\frac{1}{2}$ lb. sugar to 2 lb. fruit. Leave headspace.

Unsweetened pack. Use the same method as dry sugar pack, but omit the sugar.

Syrup Pack. Make a 40% syrup (*see* p. 62). Quarter fill containers with cold syrup, and slice apples directly into containers. Press fruit down and, if necessary, add syrup to cover. Leave headspace.

Many people prefer to blanch apple slices in boiling water for 2–3 minutes or in steam 3–5 minutes before packing by any of the above methods.

APPLE SAUCE

Cook peeled, cored and sliced apples to a pulp with a minimum of water. The best way of doing this is in a casserole in the oven. Strain off any water, and mash. Sweeten to taste and cool in a basin over cold water. Leave headspace.

APRICOTS

Choose firm, ripe, evenly coloured apricots. Wipe fruit but do not peel. Cut into halves and remove stones. Work quickly and with small quantities to avoid discoloration.

Dry Sugar Pack. To prevent discoloration pour 1,000 milligrams of ascorbic acid dissolved in $\frac{1}{2}$ cup of cold water over each 2 lb. of fruit. Add sugar to fruit at the rate of $\frac{1}{2}$ cup per pound, either during packing or before. Leave headspace.

Syrup Pack. Use a 40% syrup. Pack fruit into containers and cover with syrup. Leave headspace.

BILBERRIES (Wortleberries)

Use the unsweetened pack if the bilberries are to be used for cooking: if to be served uncooked use a syrup pack.

Unsweetened Pack. Put bilberries into containers, leaving headspace.

Syrup Pack. Put bilberries into containers and cover with a 40–50% syrup. Leave headspace.

BLACKBERRIES

Avoid blackberries with large, woody pips.

Unsweetened Pack. Pack prepared blackberries into containers, leaving headspace.

Dry Sugar Pack. To each 2 lb. fruit, add ½ lb. sugar, mixing until the fruit is well coated. Leave headspace.

Syrup Pack. Use a 50% syrup. Pack fruit into containers and cover with syrup. Leave headspace.

CHERRIES, sour

Pit the cherries. The stones tend to flavour the fruit during storage.

Dry Sugar Pack. Add and mix ½ lb. sugar with each 2 lb. pitted cherries. Leave headspace.

Syrup Pack. Make a 50% or heavier syrup, put pitted cherries in containers and cover with syrup. Leave headspace.

CHERRIES, sweet

Red varieties are better than black for freezing. Pit the cherries, pack them into containers and cover with a 40% syrup. Leave headspace.

CURRANTS, Red and Black

Top and tail currants, then wash and drain them.

Unsweetened Pack. Pack, leaving headspace. This pack can be used for jelly and preserve-making later on.

Dry Sugar Pack. Use 1 part in volume of sugar to 3 parts berries. Mix until most of the sugar is dissolved. Pack, leaving headspace.

Syrup Pack. Pack berries into their containers and cover them with a 40–50% syrup, depending on taste. Leave headspace.

DAMSONS

A tendency for the skins to toughen and the stone to flavour the fruit makes long storage impractical. It is recommended that damsons should either be stored in purée form or packed unsweetened for a short time for subsequent cheese, jam or pie-making.

GOOSEBERRIES

Select ripe berries and top and tail them.

Gooseberries may be packed unsweetened, or packed and covered with a 50% (or heavier) syrup. In either case, leave headspace.

GRAPES

Select the type of grape you enjoy eating. Avoid grapes with tough skins. Cut grapes in half and remove pips. Pipless grapes may be frozen whole.

Grapes may be packed unsweetened, or packed into containers and covered with a 40% syrup. Leave headspace.

GREENGAGES

Use method given for plums.

LOGANBERRIES

Use method given for blackberries.

NECTARINES

Use method given for peaches.

PEACHES

Choose fully ripe peaches. If they can be peeled without being plunged into boiling water so much the better. If not, put in boiling water for 30 seconds and then into cold water; this will loosen the skins.

Dry Sugar Pack. Slice fruit adding sugar at the rate of

1 part in volume of sugar to each 3 parts peach slices. Mix well and pack into containers, leaving headspace.

Syrup Pack. Part-fill containers with 40% cold syrup and slice peaches directly into them. Press fruit well down and cover with syrup. Leave headspace.

PEARS

Pears do not freeze very well as a rule. Choose ripe, but not over-ripe, pears with a strong flavour for the best results.

Make a 40% syrup and bring it to the boil. Put a wire basket into boiling syrup and slice the peeled pears into this. Cook them 1–1½ minutes. Drain and cool. Put pears into containers and cover them with a *cold* 40% syrup. Leave headspace.

PINEAPPLE

Skin and cut into slices or chunks. Throw away core.

Pineapple may be packed unsweetened, or syrup-packed in a 40% or weaker syrup. Leave headspace.

PLUMS

Plums (and greengages) may be deep-frozen whole (the tendency of stones to flavour fruit will shorten storage life), or cut into halves or smaller sizes, and stoned.

Unsweetened Pack. Small, whole fruit may be packed into containers. Leave headspace. The skin is inclined to toughen with this method.

Syrup Pack. Cut and stone fruit. Part-fill containers with a 50% syrup and put fruit in containers, pressing it down and finally topping up with syrup. Leave headspace.

RASPBERRIES

Take care not to bruise the fruit when washing, and drain carefully.

Unsweetened Pack. Put raspberries into the containers. Leave headspace.

Dry Sugar Pack. Juice will run when sugar is added, so treat this as a "wet" pack and if possible, use a rigid container. Use 1 part in volume of sugar to 4 parts berries. Either mix sugar and berries in a bowl before putting into containers, or alternate fruit and sugar (in that order) when packing. Leave headspace.

Syrup Pack. Use a cold 40% syrup. Pack berries into their containers and cover with syrup. Leave headspace.

RHUBARB

It is important to choose young rhubarb and freeze it early in the season—preferably before it needs skinning.

Trim and cut stalks into 1–2-inch pieces, or longer pieces if these are preferred. Colour and flavour retention are assisted if rhubarb is dropped into boiling water for 1 minute, then into cold water to cool, and drained, but this is not essential.

Unsweetened Pack. Pack into containers and leave headspace.

Syrup Pack. Put rhubarb into containers and cover with a 40–50% syrup. Leave headspace.

STRAWBERRIES

Strawberries are best frozen dry although the other methods are possible. Two varieties of strawberries are now known to be the best for freezing, Cambridge Vigour and Cambridge Favourite.

Unsweetened Pack. Pack clean, dry fruit into containers, leaving headspace.

Dry Sugar Pack. Put whole, crushed or sliced strawberries into a bowl and add 1 part in volume of sugar to

69

every 4 parts fruit. Mix thoroughly by tossing gently in bowl. Pack in containers, leaving headspace.

Syrup Pack. Pack strawberries in container and cover with cold 40% syrup. Leave headspace.

FRUIT PURÉES

Fruit purées are extremely easy to make and freeze. Ripe, but not over-ripe, fruit should be used.

Trim and wash and reject any that is bruised. If the fruit is soft enough to be put straight through a sieve or food mill, pulp it in this way, but don't push through the "dregs". Even strawberry "pips" are best left outside the purée.

Plums, damsons, greengages, etc., should be put in a casserole in the oven to start the juice running before being sieved.

Mix the purée with as much sugar as you would use if you intended to eat it at once. Pack, leaving headspace, seal and freeze.

If a "cooked" purée is preferred, prepare it in the normal way, then *cool*, pack, seal (leaving headspace) and freeze.

FRUIT JUICES

Tomatoes. Quarter washed tomatoes and put in a saucepan over gentle heat. When tomatoes are pulped and boiling, remove from heat and put through a sieve. Cool juice in a basin placed in cold water. Add salt to taste, pack in containers. Leave headspace and seal.

Apple. Wash the apples, remove the stalks and check for scab on skin. Cut the fruit into quarters, and put into a large saucepan, allowing ½ pint of water to each 2 lb. of apples. Simmer until tender, then carefully strain the juice, cool thoroughly and pack into containers, polythene bags or plastic tubs. It can also be frozen in ice-cream cube trays,

70

and if this is done the frozen cubes can be knocked out and packed for storage in polythene bags. Apple skins left after using the fruit for pies can also be used for making apple juice. Add water to the peelings, simmer, then strain and pack as above. It is best not to add sugar to apple juice before freezing as it quickly starts to ferment, sweetening can always be added afterwards in the proportions required.

Apple Mint. While the apples are cooking add a big bunch of washed mint sprigs to the liquid, let them remain in the pan until a strong mint flavour develops, then use the juice in the same way as given above. This makes a good addition to fruit punches and other drinks.

Berry and other Fruits. This method can be used for any fruit except citrus ones.

Wash the fruit, checking carefully for defects or insects, mash soft fruits with a potato masher or a silver fork. Add 1 cup of water to each 4 cups of fruit. Simmer for 10 minutes, then strain through a clean cloth or jelly bag, and let it cool. Sweeten to taste, if liked, or sweeten some and leave some without sugar. Fill into any moisture-proof container, leaving $\frac{1}{2}$-inch headspace. This can also be frozen in ice-cube trays and packed into polythene bags.

This fruit juice can be used for desserts, jellies, fruit drinks or just as an addition to fruit pies instead of water.

Citrus Fruits. Squeeze the juice from the fruits, heat to boiling point, cool quickly and then freeze. If the juice is not cooled before freezing it is apt to curdle and needs vigorously stirring when thawed.

COMMERCIAL OR CATERING PACKS

It is often possible to buy large tins of such fruits as peaches and apricots or mandarin oranges, which do not normally appear fresh in this country, very much more cheaply than in the small sizes. You can then open the tins, divide the contents into the sort of amounts you would ordinarily use, pack into cartons and seal. Ask your grocer to get these packs for you if he does not normally stock them.

Eggs, Cream, Butter, Ice-cream and Cheese

Eggs should not be frozen in their shells, because the shells will crack.

WHOLE EGGS

Break eggs into a bowl and beat. Beaten whole egg is inclined to become rather thick: to avoid this add ¾ teaspoonful of salt or 2 tablespoonfuls of sugar to each cup of beaten egg. Note which you have done on the package.

EGG YOLKS

These will coagulate considerably unless pre-treated with 1 teaspoonful of salt, or 2 tablespoonfuls of sugar to each cup of beaten egg yolks.

EGG WHITES

Do not beat. No pre-freezing treatment is needed.

3 tablespoonfuls yolks and whites = 1 egg
2 tablespoonfuls white = 1 egg white
1 tablespoonful yolk = 1 egg yolk

PACKING

The general rule is to pack eggs in usable quantities, leaving headspace for expansion.

Small quantities of egg prepared for the freezer may be put in small bags and sealed, and a number of these bags put into a larger bag or carton.

Another method of packing usable quantities is to put the prepared eggs into a plastic ice-cube tray, similar to those supplied with modern refrigerators. Once they are frozen, the cubes of egg may be extracted and packed in a heat-sealing bag of moisture-vapour-proof material. Each cube, or a usable quantity of cubes, may be sealed off into separate compartments in the bag with a pair of warm curling tongs, but be sure to put a barrier of paper between the tongs and the bag. If this method is used, it is easy to cut off the quantity of egg cubes needed, while leaving a well-sealed container which may be safely returned to the freezer.

THAWING

Thaw eggs in their unopened containers at room temperature, or in a refrigerator.

Thawed egg yolks and whole eggs should be used immediately. Egg whites will keep for a day or two if they are stored in a refrigerator.

CREAM

Low butterfat cream is not suitable for deep-frozen storage as it tends to separate, but creams containing 40–60% butterfat may be frozen and stored satisfactorily for periods up to 4 months.

Cream for the freezer, other than Devonshire and Cornish cream which is heat-treated in its preparation, should be first pasteurized and then cooled rapidly to 50°F. Cream should be packed in leak-proof, moisture-proof containers, leaving 1-inch headspace for expansion. It is essential that cream destined for the freezer should be prepared and frozen quickly. Cream from the top of the milk bottle can be frozen, but for use it must be beaten and served as whipped cream.

ICE-CREAM

Both bought and home-made ice-cream may be stored in the deep-freezer for 3–4 months. The better the ingredients, the longer the ice-cream will retain its flavour and texture.

Store bought ice-cream in its original container, making sure that it is fully frozen before being put in the freezer. It is a mistake to put in bought ice-cream packages which have already begun to thaw, but if slight thawing is inevitable, wrap any carton that might leak in moisture-vapour-proof paper before putting it in the freezer.

The best home-made ice-cream for the freezer is one made with pure cream and gelatine or egg yolks, and prepared in an ice-cream freezer. If ice-cream is made too slowly it will be grainy and will not lose this texture during storage.

Pack the ice-cream in leak-proof, moisture-vapour-proof containers in usable quantities and freeze quickly.

Ice-cream for parties may be put in shaped moulds, and wrapped and stored in the freezer.

Water ices may also be made and stored in the deep freezer.

BUTTER

Unsalted butter made from pasteurized cream will keep in the deep freezer for about a year. Salt butter keeps for about 6 months. Sour-cream butter will keep only for a very short period.

Bought butter may be stored in its original packing, so long as it is firm. If it is soft, the packet should be overwrapped. Home-made butter should be packed in cartons or wrapped in moisture-vapour-proof paper.

CHEESE

Cream cheeses do not make a satisfactory deep-frozen product, but hard cheeses keep well for 4–6 months providing they are correctly packed. The blue cheeses, Danish, Roquefort, etc., are inclined to be rather crumbly after being stored in the deep freezer.

Allow cheese to mature to that stage of ripeness which is pleasing, or buy it at this stage. Cut the cheese into quantities which will be eaten quickly, and pack in moisture-vapour-proof paper. It is most important to observe all the rules of packing and to seal carefully to avoid drying out during storage and cross-contamination.

Bread, Cakes, Sandwiches and Pastry

There is nothing to be said in favour of freezing for the sake of freezing, but there is everything to be said—and said enthusiastically—for making each baking day a slightly larger operation, so that some of its products can go into the deep freezer. This will extend the interval between baking days and be more economical with fuel.

UNCOOKED YEAST BREAD

Unbaked yeast breads and rolls may be frozen, but quality is inclined to vary. Unbaked yeast doughs should not be stored for longer than 2 weeks.

Prepare dough and allow it to rise. The dough may then be shaped or, if bulk freezing is preferred, flattened after one rising. Coating the surfaces with a good olive oil or melted *fresh* butter retards toughening of the crust. Sweetened recipes should have a little extra sugar added to them when the dough is to be frozen.

Pack single loaves in moisture-vapour-proof paper and seal. If packing a quantity of rolls, separate each layer with two sheets of transparent paper before overall wrapping with moisture-vapour-proof material and sealing.

Thawing. Thaw shaped bread and rolls in a moist, warm place. The more rapid the thawing, the better the loaf. Dough frozen in bulk should be first thawed, then shaped. Put thawed bread and rolls to rise in a warm place, then bake as usual.

COOKED YEAST BREAD AND ROLLS

Cooked, frozen yeast bread and rolls store much more satisfactorily than uncooked yeast doughs.

Prepare and bake the breads and rolls according to your usual recipe. Cool as quickly as possible after baking. Wrap and seal in moisture-vapour-proof paper.

Thawing. Thaw bread at room temperature.

It is best to thaw and heat *rolls* in a slow to moderate oven for 10–20 minutes according to size. Use thawed and heated rolls at once, for they become stale very rapidly. In case of emergencies it can be an advantage to have half a loaf frozen. This can then be taken from the freezer and put under the grill with the cut surface up. By the time it is toasted a slice can be cut off and toasted on the other side, while the half-loaf is again placed under the grill.

BREAD AND SCONES MADE WITH BAKING POWDER

These may be made and frozen before or after cooking. If frozen *before* cooking they should not be kept in the deep freezer for longer than 2 weeks. If frozen *after* cooking storage "life" is extended to about 2 months.

Thawing. Unbaked scones and breads may be cooked in a hot oven without thawing, or partially thawed and then cooked.

Pre-cooked scones and breads may be partially thawed and then warmed up in a moderate oven.

BISCUITS

There is little point in freezing biscuits that are cooked for they will keep well in air-tight tins. On the other hand, many uncooked biscuit mixtures will keep for as long as 6 months, and it is well worth while preparing some extra mixture for storage while baking.

The most satisfactory biscuit mixtures are those rich in fat but low in moisture.

Prepare the mixture and pack in usable quantities in moisture-vapour-proof material, seal and freeze.

Thawing. It will be necessary to thaw the mixture so that it can be rolled and shaped. Cook in the same way as fresh biscuits.

CAKES

Cakes baked before freezing keep well for 2–4 months. Uncooked cakes should not be kept for longer than 1–2 months. Fat-free sponge cakes without icing may be stored for as long as 10 months.

Ordinary recipes may be used, but synthetic vanilla should be avoided.

ICINGS AND FILLINGS

Boiled icing and cream fillings should not be used as they crumble after storage. Egg-white icings should also be avoided because they dry out. Fruit fillings will make the cake soggy. It is better to add jam to sponges after they are thawed.

The most satisfactory icing for cakes to be frozen is an uncooked butter icing made with *fresh* butter and icing sugar.

Packing. Pack cooked cakes in moisture-vapour-proof material and seal. If there is any risk of breaking, put the cakes in boxes.

Uncooked cake batter must be packed in a rust-proof tin—preferably that in which it will ultimately be cooked—wrapped in moisture-vapour-proof material and sealed.

Cooked cup cakes may be packed in a carton with a piece of transparent paper between each layer, the whole wrapped in moisture-vapour-proof material and sealed.

Thawing. Thaw plain cakes—i.e. cakes without icing—at room temperature. Thaw iced cakes in a refrigerator or very cool larder and keep them there until they are served. If iced remove wrapping material before thawing.

Thaw cake batter at room temperature and cook as soon as it is thawed.

SANDWICHES

A number of fillings can be used for sandwiches that are to be frozen—sliced cooked meat, cheese, peanut butter, meat spreads and sardines, but some fillings should be avoided.

Make the sandwiches in the usual way and wrap in usable amounts in moisture-vapour-proof material, seal and freeze.

Sandwiches should not be kept in frozen storage for longer than 1 month. Open sandwiches should not be kept longer than 2 weeks.

DO NOT USE: *hard-boiled egg* because the white will become leathery; *jam* because it may seep; *"crisp" fillings* such as *lettuce, celery, tomato, cucumber*, because they will become soggy during storage, or when thawed; *mayonnaise or sandwich spreads containing mayonnaise* because they may curdle during storage.

BOX-LUNCHES

The deep freezer can be used in the partial or total preparation of box-lunches.

Separate items such as sandwiches, small cakes and fruit may be frozen and then assembled as needed.

Sandwiches and small cakes will thaw in about 2 hours after being removed from the deep freezer. If *fresh* tomatoes or lettuce are available, they can be put into the lunch box when it is packed to go out, and the thawing foods from the deep freezer will keep them crisp and fresh.

PASTRY

For mechanical reasons, pastry dough frozen in bulk

is not very satisfactory. It takes a long time to thaw, and is inclined to crumble when being rolled. If rolled before freezing it becomes brittle during storage. The best way of storing frozen dough is rolled out in flan cases, but unless equal-sized flan cases are used and storage placing carefully planned, there will be a considerable waste of space. It is more economical to prepare complete pastry dishes for the freezer.

Apart from custard fillings, which separate, and pies covered with meringue, which toughens or dries out during storage, most standard recipes can be used for deep and shallow covered pies.

Uncooked Pies. Frozen, uncooked pastry usually tastes better than frozen cooked pastry. Make the pie, but do not put air vents in the top crust before freezing. For pies with pastry top and bottom, brush the inner side of the pastry with egg white to prevent juices seeping into the pastry. Wrap the pie and its plate (*which must be rust-proof and crack-proof at* $-5°F$) in moisture-vapour-proof material, seal and freeze.

It is unnecessary to thaw uncooked fruit pies. Unwrap them and cut vents in the top crust. Cook for about fifteen minutes longer than the time allowed for a similar fresh pie. Pies other than fruit pies should be allowed to thaw at room temperature before cooking.

Cooked Pies. Cook the pie in the normal way and cool it. It should be packed with its plate or dish, which must be rust-proof and crack-proof, at $-5°F$. Wrap in moisture-vapour-proof material, seal and freeze. Thaw at room temperature, or in a slow oven.

It is important to leave room for expansion between fruit and pastry when making a deep fruit, or similar type of pie.

Ready-cooked Foods

There is no limit to the number of emergencies for which a supply of ready-cooked food in the deep freezer can be useful. Unexpected guests, harvest time, school holidays, workmen in the house, Christmas, birthdays—all the cooking preparation for these events can be undertaken in advance, so that when the time comes catering and cooking problems are minimized.

On a more everyday basis, possession of a deep freezer permits planned catering to cover several weeks—bigger but less frequent bakings. Whole meals may be prepared and cooked and put into the freezer, but don't do this without some plan in mind, thinking they will come in handy one day, some day. Pre-cooked food has a short storage "life" (*see* Storage tables, p. 88). Apart from this, the shorter time pre-cooked food is stored the better, for fats tend to become rancid, and all foods undergo a gradual loss of flavour, aroma and texture. Long storage of pre-cooked food, even when it isn't dangerous, can result in food that tempts the eye but disappoints the palate.

Pre-cooked frozen food is a great field for experiment. Don't be afraid to try. Practically all cooked foods can be frozen, but some will yield a better product for the table than others. Observe these general directions.

GENERAL DIRECTIONS

1. Use good raw materials, avoiding the addition of those unsuitable for freezing.
2. Observe every rule of hygiene during preparation.

3. Do not overcook.
4. Cool thoroughly and quickly.
5. Pack and seal.
6. Label with date.
7. Freeze.

THINGS TO AVOID

1. Starchy things such as potatoes, macaroni, spaghetti and rice in stews, soups, sauces, etc. These incline to become mushy, or acquire a warmed-up flavour when thawed and reheated. Such starchy foods may be cooked freshly and added to frozen stews and soups while they are being reheated.
2. Hard-boiled eggs. The whites become leathery during storage.
3. Mayonnaise, because it curdles.

POINTS TO REMEMBER

Dishes containing milk or cheese tend to separate or curdle during thawing but sometimes recombine if they can be beaten.

Fried foods become rancid quickly and tend to have a reheated flavour.

Fats tend to separate in gravies, stews and sauces. It is essential to remove excess fat before freezing.

Thickened sauces and gravies thicken still more during storage; use cornflour instead of ordinary flour as a thickening agent.

Most seasonings become stronger during storage, so should be limited, or added while reheating.

All pre-cooked foods should be used within recommended storage period.

SOUPS

Most soups freeze satisfactorily. The exceptions, which have varying results, are those containing milk or cream. Potatoes, barley, macaroni, spaghetti, rice and other starchy foods should be added to the soups *after* frozen storage; in frozen storage they become soggy.

Method:
1. Make soup, avoiding ingredients mentioned in opening paragraph.
2. Strain through a fine strainer. If necessary use cheese-cloth.
3. Cool.
4. Remove all surplus fat.
5. Pack in water-tight, moisture-vapour-proof containers.
6. Leave $\frac{1}{2}$-inch headspace per pint for wide-topped and $\frac{3}{4}$-inch for narrow-topped containers respectively.
7. Seal, label and freeze.

SOUPS SHOULD NOT BE STORED FOR LONGER THAN 2 MONTHS.

Thawing. Thaw clear soups in a saucepan over a low flame. Thaw cream soups in a double boiler. If cream soup curdles, vigorous beating may restore smoothness.

COOKED MEAT AND POULTRY

The most practical cooked meat and poultry dishes for deep-frozen storage are those which take a considerable time to cook. There is little point in freezing a cooked steak or chop, or a piece of fried chicken, when a better result comes from using fresh meats or freezing it raw, and only a few minutes' cooking time is required.

MEAT AND POULTRY DISHES WITHOUT SAUCES

Cook according to a standard recipe, but be careful not to overcook.

Minimize seasonings, or omit them altogether and add during reheating.

Remember that if meat or poultry is stuffed, its satisfactory storage "life" is shortened to that of the stuffing.

Cool food very thoroughly.

Pack "dry" cooked meat and poultry—i.e. without sauces and gravies—in moisture-vapour-proof paper, overwrapping if necessary, and seal.

Label and date.

Freeze.

Thawing. Thaw cooked "dry" meats in their containers.

STEWS AND COMBINATION DISHES

The quality of the frozen combination dish depends on the reaction of its ingredients to deep-frozen storage. It is important to omit ingredients which are known to store badly. It is also important not to overcook, for most combination dishes are intended for reheating later.

Omit:

Potatoes, macaroni, rice, spaghetti and all such starchy ingredients. These do not freeze well and may be added fresh during reheating.

85

Hard-boiled egg. The white becomes leathery during storage.

Excessive seasoning. Seasoning becomes stronger during storage.

Mayonnaise.

Stews and combination dishes should be cooled thoroughly and quickly, remembering that this type of food is most susceptible to attack by bacteria.

Pack stews and combination dishes in rigid (rust-proof and crack-proof at −5°F), water-tight, moisture-vapour-proof containers, leaving 1-inch headspace. Seal and freeze.

Thawing. Dishes which are to be eaten cold should be thawed in their containers. Do this in the coolest place available. Thawing at room temperature may cause deterioration if it takes longer than 4 hours.

Dishes which require reheating may be unwrapped and reheated in the oven, or in a double boiler. It is important to restrain the heat to avoid overcooking. The oven should be low, or the water below a double boiler only warm to begin with, otherwise there is a risk of sticking.

LEFT-OVERS

If left-overs are to be frozen they must be done quickly.

Slice left-over meat and pack the slices together compactly before wrapping and sealing.

Wrap left-over cakes and tarts carefully and seal.

Put soup into a water-tight, moisture-vapour-proof container, leaving headspace, and seal.

Left-over vegetables do not freeze satisfactorily.

Left-overs which have already been in deep-frozen storage should not be re-frozen.

Left-overs should not be stored for longer than 2 weeks.

SAUCES

Sauces for special dishes may be prepared and frozen, so long as the general directions are followed, and ingredients which store poorly are avoided. In general, sauces containing little fat are more satisfactory than sauces rich in fat. All excess fat must be removed before packing. When packing, remember to use a water-tight container and leave headspace for expansion.

Frozen Food Suppliers

Since this book was first published, a number of firms have started specialising in supplying commercially frozen food in bulk at almost wholesale prices.

The advantages of such a service to the town housewife who is not able to freeze her own home-grown produce hardly need stressing: buying food in this way not only reduces the time spent on daily or weekly shopping, but it also means considerable saving on household bills.

Most firms selling everyday fare such as meat and vegetables will also be able to supply food for special occasions: smoked salmon, prawns, scallops, asparagus and even cakes and pastries.

When choosing a frozen food supplier, it is a good idea to make sure the goods are packaged in a sensible manner. Portions of meat or vegetables should be packed in such a way that small quantities can be easily removed from the freezer.

If you have difficulty in getting in touch with bulk suppliers of commercially frozen food you can obtain details of suppliers in your area from either of the following sources:

The Food Freezer Council,
73–76 Jermyn Street,
London, S.W.1.

The Electricity Council.
Trafalgar Buildings,
1 Charing Cross,
London, S.W.1.

(Stored at −5°F or below)

	14 days	1 or less	1–2	2–3	3–4	4–6	6–8	8–10	10–12
Bacon, sliced	.	☆	.	.	.	.	.	.	.
Beef	.	.	.	.	.	.	.	.	☆
Biscuit Mixture uncooked	.	.	.	.	.	☆	.	.	.
Bread and Rolls									
cooked, yeast	.	.	.	☆	.	.	.	.	.
uncooked, yeast	☆	.	.	.	.	.	.	.	.
Bread and Scones									
cooked, baking powder	.	.	☆	.	.	.	.	.	.
uncooked, baking powder	☆	.	.	.	.	.	.	.	.
Butter									
fresh	.	.	.	.	.	.	.	.	☆
salted	.	.	.	.	.	☆	.	.	.
Cakes									
cooked	.	.	.	.	☆	.	.	.	.
uncooked	.	.	☆	.	.	.	.	.	.
fat-free, cooked sponge, no icing	.	.	.	.	.	.	.	☆	.
Cheese	.	.	.	.	.	☆	.	.	.
Crab	.	☆	.	.	.	.	.	.	.
Cream	.	.	.	.	☆	.	.	.	.
Duck	.	.	.	.	.	☆	.	.	.
Eels	.	.	.	☆	.	.	.	.	.
Eggs	.	.	.	.	.	.	☆	.	.
Fish									
fatty	.	.	.	☆	.	.	.	.	.
lean	.	.	.	.	☆	.	.	.	.
Flounder	.	.	.	.	☆	.	.	.	.
Fruit									
citrus	.	.	.	.	.	☆	.	.	.
non-citrus in sugar or syrup	.	.	.	.	.	.	.	.	☆
without sugar or syrup	.	.	.	.	.	.	.	☆	.
Fruit Juices									
citrus	.	.	.	.	.	☆	.	.	.
non-citrus	.	.	.	.	.	.	.	☆	.
Fruit Purees	.	.	.	.	.	.	☆	.	.
Game Birds	.	.	.	.	.	.	☆	.	.
Giblets	.	.	.	☆	.	.	.	.	.
Goose	.	.	.	.	.	☆	.	.	.
Gravies	.	.	☆	.	.	.	.	.	.
Halibut	.	.	.	☆	.	.	.	.	.
Ham	.	.	.	.	☆	.	.	.	.
Hare	.	.	.	.	.	.	☆	.	.

(Stored at − 5°F or below)

	14 days	1 or less	1–2	2–3	3–4	4–6	6–8	8–10	10–12
HEART	.	.	.	.	☆	.	.	.	.
HERRING	.	.	.	☆	.	.	.	.	.
ICE-CREAM	.	.	.	.	☆	.	.	.	.
KIDNEYS	.	.	.	.	☆	.	.	.	.
LAMB	.	.	.	.	.	.	☆	.	.
LEFT-OVER cooked food	☆	.	.	.	.	.	.	.	.
LIVER	.	.	.	☆	.	.	.	.	.
LOBSTER	.	☆	.	.	.	.	.	.	.
MACKEREL	.	.	☆	.	.	.	.	.	.
MINCE unseasoned	.	.	.	.	☆	.	.	.	.
OYSTERS	.	☆	.	.	.	.	.	.	.
PIES, uncooked	.	.	☆	.	.	.	.	.	.
PLAICE	.	.	.	.	☆	.	.	.	.
PORK	.	.	.	.	.	.	☆	.	.
POULTRY unstuffed	.	.	.	.	.	.	.	.	☆
stuffed	.	.	☆	.	.	.	.	.	.
PRAWNS	.	☆	.	.	.	.	.	.	.
RABBIT	.	.	.	.	.	.	☆	.	.
READY-COOKED MEAT DISHES	.	.	☆	.	.	.	.	.	.
SALMON	.	.	.	☆	.	.	.	.	.
SANDWICHES closed	.	☆	.	.	.	.	.	.	.
open	☆	.	.	.	.	.	.	.	.
SAUCES	.	.	☆	.	.	.	.	.	.
SAUSAGES unseasoned and unsalted	.	.	.	.	.	☆	.	.	.
seasoned and salted	.	☆	.	.	.	.	.	.	.
SHRIMPS	.	☆	.	.	.	.	.	.	.
SOUP	.	.	☆	.	.	.	.	.	.
STUFFINGS	.	.	☆	.	.	.	.	.	.
TARTS, uncooked	.	.	.	☆	.	.	.	.	.
TONGUE	.	.	.	.	☆	.	.	.	.
TROUT	.	.	.	.	☆	.	.	.	.
TURBOT	.	.	.	☆	.	.	.	.	.
TURKEY	.	.	.	.	.	☆	.	.	.
VEAL	.	.	.	.	.	.	☆	.	.
VEGETABLES	.	.	.	.	.	.	.	.	☆
VEGETABLE PURÉES	.	.	.	.	.	.	.	☆	.
VENISON	.	.	.	.	.	.	.	☆	.
WHITING	.	.	.	.	☆	.	.	.	.

Bibliography

FREEZING FRUITS, VEGETABLES AND MEATS, by Marie C. Doermann and Walter A. Maclinn (Rutgers University, New Brunswick, N.J.).

VARIETY EVERY DAY WITH FROZEN FOODS, by Mrs. Mildred Daniel (South Dakota State College).

FROZEN FOODS (General Electric Company of America).

FOOD FREEZING QUESTIONS (General Electric Company of America).

FROZEN FOODS, PRECOOKED, PREPARED, by Mary E. Loughead (Extension Service, Montana State College).

HOME FREEZING OF FRUITS AND VEGETABLES (U.S. Department of Agriculture).

HOME FREEZING OF FOOD, by Vera Greaves Mark (University of California).

PRINCIPLES OF FOOD FREEZING, by Gorner, Erdmann and Masterman (John Wiley and Sons, New York).

HOME FREEZING OF FRUITS AND VEGETABLES
FREEZING YEAST AND QUICK BREADS, PIES, COOKIES AND CAKES } (U.S. Department of
FREEZING MEAT AND POULTRY PRODUCTS } Agriculture.)
FREEZING COMBINATION MAIN DISHES

FREEZING FOODS FOR MICHIGAN HOMES (Michigan State College).

QUICK FROZEN FOODS, by Robert Sinclair (Unilever).

DOMESTIC PRESERVATION OF MEATS AND POULTRY (Ministry of Agriculture, Fisheries and Food, H.M.S.O.).

Index

ADDITIONS to freezer, 33–4
Air extraction, 22, 30, 32
  pockets, 26–7
Apple juice, 70
  mint juice, 71
  sauce, 65
Apples, 64
Apricots, 65
Asparagus, 53

BACON, 38
Bags, 26, 31
  disadvantage, 27
  sealing, 27
  bunched, 29, 30, 32
Beans, broad, 53
  French, 53
  runner, 53
Beetroot, 54
Berry and other juices, 71
Bilberries, 65
Biscuits, 78
Blackberries, 65
Blanching, 50–1
Box lunches, 80
Bread, 77–8
Brine packing, 52
Broccoli, 54
Brussels sprouts, 54
Butter, 75
BX Polythene film, 27

CABBAGE, 54
Cakes, 79
  fillings, 79
Carrots, 55
Cauliflower, 55
Cheese, 76
Cherries, 66

Chops, 37
Citrus fruits, 71
Combination dishes, 85
Containers, rigid, 25
Cooked meat, 84
Crab, 41
Cream, 74
Cross-contamination, 21–2
Currants, red and black, 66

DAMSONS, 66
Dating, 22
Dehydration, 24–5
Desiccation, 30–1
Discoloration of fruit, 62
  preventing, 63
Dry ice, 15
Dry sugar pack, 61, 64

EGGS, packing, 73–4
  thawing, 74
  whites, 73
  whole, 73
  yolks, 73
Expansion of food, 32

FASTENERS, plastic, 29
Fats in storage, 25
Fish, 40–2
  crab, 41
  fatty, 40
  lean, 40
  lobster, 41–2
  oysters, 42
  prawns, 42
  shrimps, 42
Flat seal, 24, 27, 29
Food selection, 18–19, 21

Freezer, cleaning, 15
  defrosting, 14
  motor, 12, 15
  power failure, 15
  price, 11
  running costs, 13–14
  size, 11, 13
  space allocation, 18
  temperature, 23
  burn, 25
Freezing, 33
Fruit, 60–72
  cooking, 64
  discoloration, 62
  dry sugar packing, 61
  headspace, 62
  juices, 70
  method, 60–1
  overripe, 21
  purées, 70
  syrup packing, 61–2
  thawing, 63
  unripe, 21
  unsweetened packing, 61

GAME, 47–9
  hanging, 49
  hares, 48
  method, 47
  rabbits, 48
  venison, 48–9
Gooseberries, 67
Grapes, 67
Greaseproof paper, 25
Greengages, 67

HAM, 38
Hares, 48
Headspace, 29, 62
Hygiene, 21

ICE-CREAM, 75
Icings, 79

KITCHEN foil, 25
Kohlrabi, 56

LABELLING, 22, 32
Left-overs, 86
Lobster, 41–2
Loganberries, 67

MARROW, 56
Meat, 35–9
  cooked, 84–5
Mince, 37
Mixed vegetables, 56
Mushrooms, 56

NECTARINES, 67

OFFAL, 37
Overwrapping, 27, 30
Oxidation, 24–5
Oysters, 42

PACKING, 19, 22, 30
  choice of, 24
  liquids, 29
  materials, 21, 22, 24, 25–6, 27, 30, 31
  papers, 25
Packs, commercial or catering, 71
Parsley, 57
Parsnips, 57
Pastry, 80–1
Peaches, 67
Pears, 68
Peas, 57
Peppers, 57
Pies, 81
Pineapple, 68
Planning, 23
Pliofilm, 27
Plums, 68
Pork fat, 36
Poultry, 43–6
  breasts, 44
  cooked, 84–5
  cooking, 45–6
  giblets, 44–5
  jointed birds, 44

Poultry, method, 43
  stuffing, 40, 43, 45
  thawing, 45–6
  whole birds, 43–4
Prawns, 42
Purées, 58, 70

QUICK freezing, 11, 33

RABBITS, 48
Raspberries, 68
Ready-cooked foods, 82–7
  directions, 82–3
  to avoid, 83
Records, 22–3, 34
Rhubarb, 69
Rigid containers, 25–6
Running costs, 13

SANDWICHES, 80
Sauces, 87
Sausages, 38
Scones, 78
Sealing, 22, 29, 32
  bags, 31
  cartons, 32
  flat, 26
  rigid containers, 25–6, 32
  tape, 26
  tubs, 32
Selection of food, 18–19, 21
Sheet wrapping, 27, 30
Shrimps, 42
Soups, 84
Spinach, 58

Steaks, 37
Stew, 85
Stewing meat, 37
Storage capacity, 11, 12, 19
  life, 20
  tables, 88–9
Strawberries, 69
Syrup packing, 61–2

TAPE sealing, 28
Turnips, 58

UNSWEETENED packing, 61, 63

VEGETABLES, 50–9
  blanching, 50–1
  brine packing, 52
  cooking, 51–2, 58–9
  directions, 53–8
  freezing, 52–3
  method, 50
  non-leafy, 52
  overripe, 21
  packing, 52
  unsuitable, 50
Venison, 48–9
Visqueen Polythene film, 27

WAXED cartons, 26
  tape sealed, 26
  with liners, 26
Waxed tubs, 26
Wrapping sealers, 27

SENATVSP
MPCAESAR
TRAIANOA
MAXIMOTR
ADDECLARA
MONSETLOCVS

THE PRACTICAL GUIDE TO

Calligraphy

Rosemary Sassoon

Mud Puddle Books

NEW YORK

The Practical Guide to Calligraphy
by Rosemary Sassoon

ISBN: 978-1-60311-028-0

This edition published in 2005 by
Mud Puddle Books, Inc.
54 W. 21st Street, Suite 601
New York, NY 10010
info@mudpuddlebooks.com

Published by arrangement with
Thames & Hudson Ltd., London

© 1982 Thames and Hudson Ltd., London

Printed in China

CONTENTS

Introduction – 6

1 Tools and materials – 8   2 Starting to work – 10

3 The construction of the letters – 12

4 The Foundational Hand – 14   5 Using the pen – 20

6 Critical analysis – 22   7 Simple layouts – 26

8 Introducing colour – 29   9 Left-handed calligraphy – 30

10 Other basic alphabets – 32

11 Combining different hands – 46   12 Flourishes – 52

13 Materials for more advanced work – 58

14 Studying and using historical hands – 60

15 Display lettering – 70   16 Brush lettering – 74

17 Preparing work for reproduction – 78

18 Calligraphy at work – 80

Acknowledgments – 96

INTRODUCTION

THE WORD CALLIGRAPHY is derived from the Greek *kalle graphe*, meaning beautiful writing. Today, however, it suggests different things to different people; at one extreme just fine handwriting, at the other a highly creative art form. The scholar can, through ancient manuscripts, study the history and development of writing as reflecting the rise and fall of civilizations, while the letterer, stone carver or typographer uses the same manuscripts searching for inspiration from the classic letter forms.

It is arguable whether calligraphy should be termed an art or a craft. It is a craft in the sense that the discipline and training of hand and eye, and the use and respect of natural materials, demand a craftsman's skill, but the skill itself is only a tool and the beginning of the creative aspect – the interpreting of the deeper meaning of the written word as a visual art form.

Whatever way the word is understood, calligraphy must essentially be *used*, otherwise learning it becomes a sterile exercise. It can be used in many ways. There is always a demand for the traditional work of a scribe: presentation lettering of all sorts, rolls of honour, family trees, heraldry and even handwritten books.

There is also an increasing need for calligraphy in commercial art and printers' studios or architects' and draughtsmen's offices. Despite the wide range of 'instant' lettering now available, designers realize that there is no substitute for the versatility of hand lettering, and are turning to the small band of experienced letterers whose skills have often been underrated or ignored.

The first part of this book, which is largely based on my own teaching experience, is intended for the beginner who wishes to

6

acquire the basic calligraphic skills and put them into practice. In it I have made use of the plain and beautiful 'Foundational Hand' which was evolved from traditional English book hands by Edward Johnston (1872–1944); this, together with a number of variations, helps to develop the basic skills before the student goes on to experiment with some of the many historical alphabets bequeathed to us from the past. A few of these are set out in the second part of the book.

I believe that by learning to analyze and group together letters comprising similar strokes, the student can make more rapid improvement both in the early stages and later on, when this method leads to a quick grasp of the angle or particular characteristic of any new hand. The inventive calligrapher will soon find means of self-expression through the choice of letter forms and the uses to which these can be put; and such creativity should, in my view, be attempted at an early stage. I have suggested a number of practical uses for calligraphy in the second part of the book and have also included advice on preparing work for reproduction, an increasingly important aspect of the calligrapher's work. By showing some examples of my own professional work, each with a specific point to make, I also hope to give a picture of the varied life of the working letterer.

Whether calligraphy is to be used for profit or pleasure, the learning methods are the same. They are neither quick nor easy but they need not be repetitive and they should certainly never become dull. The practice of calligraphy provides a freedom of expression and makes one better able to appreciate the work done by other artists and craftsmen. It will repay in full the time you give to it.

1 Tools and materials

A beginner needs very little equipment. Use an ordinary drawing board, supported on your lap, leaning it against a steady table at a comfortable writing angle. Never try to do lettering with your work flat on a table. Pin some sheets of newspaper to the board to make a resilient working surface. Use a sheet of good quality cartridge paper, kept in place by a horizontal band of elastic. Everyone has an optimum writing position and the paper should be easily movable up and down or side to side to ensure that the hand is neither cramped nor overstretched when writing.

A double pencil is the best tool to begin with. To make one, take two short pencils, pare down one side of each and fit them together so that their points are even and about 1/8 inch apart; then fasten them with adhesive tape or thread.

For lettering with a pen, round-hand nibs can be bought separately or in sets. A selection ranging from the broadest, size 0, to the narrowest, size 6, will eventually be needed. The nibs must have a slip-on reservoir to hold ink, or be used in a penholder which has a reservoir attached. Straight nibs are needed for right-handers and left oblique nibs for left-handers. Non-waterproof ink or liquid watercolour are both used for calligraphy. Waterproof Indian ink is unsuitable as it clogs the pens.

A metal ruler, a set square and a hard pencil are needed for drawing lines, a small paintbrush for feeding ink into the reservoirs, a jar of water, a soft rubber – and that is all that is necessary.

Equipment

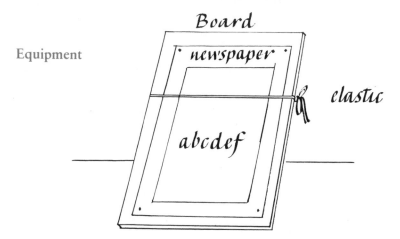

Lean the board against a table at a comfortable writing angle.
Pin a pad of newspaper to the board and tie a length of elastic to
hold the work in place.

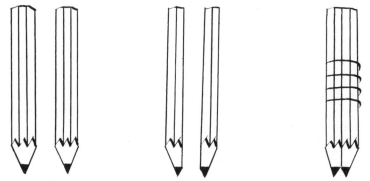

To make a double pencil, take two short pencils, pare down one
side and fasten together.

Round hand pens

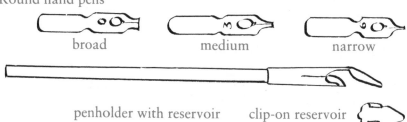

broad   medium   narrow

penholder with reservoir   clip-on reservoir

2 Starting to work

Hold the double pencil or pen in a firm, comfortable grip, so that the two points of the pencil, or the nib, are at an angle of 30° to the guide lines.

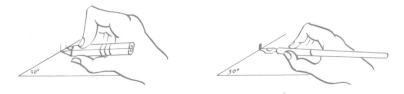

The thickest stroke will then be the diagonal from top left to bottom right, and the thinnest stroke from bottom left to top right. The upright and horizontal strokes are of medium weight.

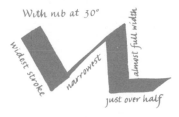

With nib at 30°

widest stroke

narrowest

almost full width

just over half

Practising the patterns that are illustrated on the opposite page, and inventing new ones, will teach control of the double pencil or pen. The writing implement must be kept at a constant angle. In the early stages it is a good idea to check the 30° occasionally with a protractor. Too sharp an angle makes the upright strokes weak, too shallow an angle makes them heavy. Accurate guidelines are essential. Correctly measured lines ensure correct weight and proportion of letter. Use a hard, sharp pencil to draw lines, and lay out your first pages with a margin and plenty of space between the sets of lines, making it easy to judge and improve your work.

Lettering is a mixture of discipline and relaxation, conformity and creativity. There are a few rules that must be followed and a plain, well-proportioned hand should be learned first. In fact 'Plain is beautiful' is a good motto for beginners.

Exercises   Double pencil   Pen

Thin upstroke left to right, thick downstroke left to right.

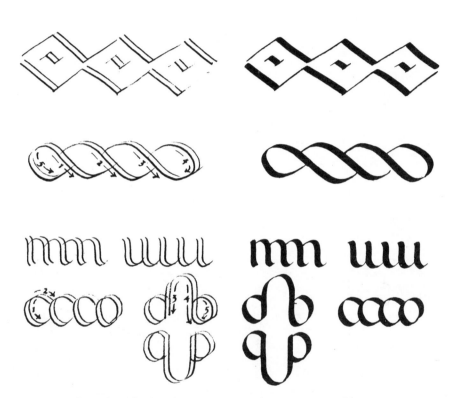

Patterns based on letter shapes are good preparation for writing.

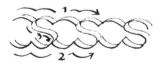 

3 The construction of the letters

When starting double pencil or pen lettering, tackle the easiest letters first. They are shown here in their simplest form, but these can be used when learning any subsequent alphabet.

iljnmrhu

iljnmrhu

First the letters constructed with straight lines and arches.

minimum

minimum

Practise words containing these letters only.

ocebdpq

ocebdpq

The letters based on the 'o' shape alone, or with upright strokes.

cope bode

cope bode

Words to practise.

agy

agy

Simplified versions of a, g and y, using the same strokes as above.

agkftz

agkftz

More complex letters and those using horizontal and diagonal strokes.

svwxy

svwxy

This non-serif alphabet is used here to analyze the shapes of letters and as a preparation for the Foundational Hand on the following pages. For instructions on guide-lines to ensure correct proportion and the order and direction of writing the strokes see p. 15.

Details and terminals of Foundational Hand small letters

Serifs (i.e. the introductory stroke at the top of the letter) neaten the upright strokes standing on their own, as in b, k and l – also i and j and the second stroke of u. Serifs are written in three separate  strokes. After the first two strokes the pen is at the correct angle for the downstroke. The top of the t also takes three strokes.

Upright strokes followed by an arch start with a slight swing left to right, as in n, m and r. An upright preceded by a curved stroke starts with an oblique right-to-left hairline. For a well-rounded arch, start the second stroke at the outer edge of the upright.

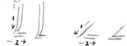

The diagonal stroke is neatened by a slight swing at the start of the stroke or a separate horizontal stroke followed by a thin diagonal.

Bases for f, k, q and p as well as x are written in two separate strokes.

Other bases are formed by a left-to-right swing at the end of the downstroke. The last stroke of multiple letters, and uprights standing alone, need larger bases to balance them.

Junctions: notice the point of the 'v' and how two curved strokes join.

4 The Foundational Hand

Guide lines for the Foundational Hand should be 4½ times the distance between the two sharpened points. Letters such as o, s and x with no ascending or descending strokes are written between these two lines. The height of these letters is called 'x height'. Notice that the ascenders and descenders of letters b, d, y, p, etc., extend to 1½ times x height. It is not necessary to draw guide lines for them. Each stroke in formal calligraphy is separate, firm and unhurried.

In the lower alphabet the separate strokes that make up each letter are numbered in the order that they should be written, and arrowed to show in which direction they should go. The pen or pencil must never be pushed or forced in the wrong direction, e.g. letters such as o, s, c, or e, which are written in one movement in our ordinary handwriting, need to be lettered in two or three separate strokes.

The double pencil will show very clearly any faults in the shape and angle of the lettering. Watch the shape of the inside of each letter as well as the outside, and keep the upright strokes steady, just turning them at the bottom to make the base.

To make an evenly spaced word, differently shaped letters need different amounts of space between them. Two round letters should be written close together, round letters followed by a straight letter need more space between them and two straight letters need most of all. If these simple rules are kept in mind, even spacing comes with practise. It is not so much a matter of measuring as of training the eye.

It is well worth spending time perfecting the shape of each letter and practising the spacing of short words, then sentences in small letters, before starting capital letters. The space between words should be the equivalent of a letter 'o'.

Small letters written with a double pencil

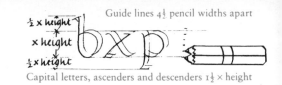

½ × height
× height
½ × height

Guide lines 4½ pencil widths apart

Capital letters, ascenders and descenders 1½ × height

a b c d e f g h i j k l m

n o p q r s t u v w

x y z   Simpler alternatives   a g y

Arrows show the direction and order in which the strokes should be written after the serif has been completed.

Foundational Hand: Capital letters

When writing capital letters only, guide lines should be 7 double pencil or pen widths apart. In general lettering, where capital letters extend to $1\frac{1}{2}$ times x height, the eye will soon manage to judge this accurately and guide lines will no longer be needed.

Make sure the strokes are written in the right order, as shown opposite, and change the angle for the third stroke of the 'N'.

To facilitate learning, Foundational Hand capital letters can be divided into sequences according to strokes and shape. They are shown here in a simple non-serif form.

Capital letters should also be studied and practised in sequences relating to their proportions:

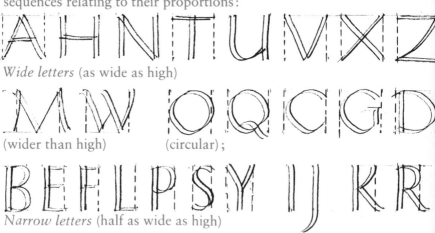

Wide letters (as wide as high)

(wider than high)   (circular);

Narrow letters (half as wide as high)

Foundational Hand:
Capital letters written with
a double pencil

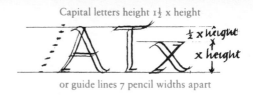

17

start

large

Measure the guide lines carefully
each time the double pencil is
re-sharpened

as you im-

prove reduce

the size by paring

more from inside

both pencils

In this example words are emphasized by shading in the lettering

A page of double pencil work by Edward Johnston (reduced).
Reproduced by kind permission of Dorothy Mahoney.

5 Using the pen

Choose a broad nib to start with. Fit the pen nib into the penholder and hold it up to the light to check that the split in the nib is not being forced open by too much pressure from the reservoir, which should just touch the inside of the nib.

Use a brush to feed some ink into the reservoir but do not overfill. Avoid dipping the pen into the inkpot because this can easily flood the nib. When using a broad nib you may need to refill with ink after every three or four letters. Support your hand on a small sheet of paper in order to keep your work clean, and to test your pen on each time it is filled.

Draw the guide lines for small letters $4\frac{1}{2}$ pen widths apart. Two or more lines of writing must be spaced at least $1\frac{1}{2}$ times this measurement apart to allow room for ascending and descending strokes. Lines consisting only of capital letters can be spaced closer together. Practise the letters in the sequences shown on page 12, not in alphabetical order. The serifs and bases of letters must be clear and sharp. The flick of the pen, either freely upwards or edged downwards, terminating strokes, will come with practise and must not be exaggerated. Firm uprights and horizontals, and keeping the pen at a consistent angle, are more important in the early stages.

Numerals are usually written with the even numbers extending above the line and the odd numbers below the line, only o and 1 are between the guidelines. The tails of the descending numbers and the top of 6 need only the inner edge of pen or pencil to follow through and finish off the stroke.

Foundational Hand
alphabet written
with a pen

Capital letters, descenders and descenders 1½ x height

abcdefghijklm
nopqrstuvw
xyz?., Simpler alternatives agy

ABCDEFG
HIJKLMN
OPQRSTU
VWXYZ&
1234567890

6 Critical analysis

It is important to know how to criticize, to analyze the faults, and to repeat a piece of lettering until it improves, keeping earlier copies for comparison.

Below is a reduction of a poem (one of Ariel's songs from Shakespeare's 'The Tempest') that I wrote out when I was a student. It was the third attempt. I have used words from all three copies in the analysis (on p. 24). The writing is already sharp and rhythmic with fairly firm uprights. However, there are still typical examples of poorly formed letters and unevenly spaced words on every line. Taking the poem line by line gives an idea of how closely lettering can be scrutinized. Look at the o's: they vary in shape. Many of the e's are too sharply angled, and the s's present problems of shape and spacing. Judging where to start an s so that its last stroke just touches the preceding letter is the sort of thing that comes only with practise. Some of the hairlines are exaggerated and the odd upright slants forward. A few letters are either too large or too small.

Full fathom five thy father lies
Of his bones are corals made
Those are pearls that were his eyes
Nothing of him that doth fade
But do suffer a sea change
Into something rich and strange
Sea nymphs hourly ring his knell
Hark now I do hear them
Ding, dong bell

Full fathom five thy father lies

falling forward
below the line *below the line* *too close*

Of his bones are corals made

too close *poor join* *slanting* *too close*

Those are pearls that were his eyes

below the line *too angled* *base too small* *sloping forward* *too close*

Nothing of him that doth fade

too close *below line* *too angled* *narrow*

But do suffer a sea change

hair lines exaggerated
narrow *too angled*

Into something rich and strange

slightly too close *this is the best written line*

Sea nymphs hourly ring his knell

too angled *poor join* *too close & narrow* *wide* *too close*

Hark now I do hear them

small base *cramped & heavy* *too angled* *sloping forward*

Ding, dong bell

short
too angled *sloping*

23

The capital letters are unsteady and of a less good standard than the rest of the lettering, as is usual in beginners' work.

Some of the better words produced in the same size as the original.

something rich

hourly   coral

knell   strange

These examples show how letters can be modified in different combinations and how others can be linked to make the spacing more even and the writing flow.

is suffer fa hy

eyes   are   hear

This is a later exercise (reduced) with slightly more even spacing and with the letters more upright and better formed. However, there are some ugly collisions of ascenders and descenders that require replanning or more widely spaced lines. The capital letters are still unsteady, and the s's are again causing trouble, except at the beginning of words. The o's and e's are improved.

Had I the heavens' embroidered cloths,
Enwrought with golden and silver light,
The blue and the dim and the dark cloths
Of night and light and the half light,
I would spread the cloths under your feet:
But I, being poor, have only my dreams;
I have spread my dreams under your feet;
Tread softly, because you tread on my dreams.

Notice how the r's are flicked up at the end of words or before a round stroke, but downwards before an upright stroke ('dark'). Even small variations give a different pattern and character to the piece.

light, cloth under
embroidered dark

As your hand improves you may reduce the size of the lettering by using a smaller nib.

7 Simple layouts

Certain decisions must be taken even before pencil is put to paper –
approximately what size is desired and whether a horizontal or
vertical layout suits the subject matter. Then a series of thumb-nail
sketches in pencil should be done, roughly indicating the title,
block or blocks of text, number of words in a line, and any
decorative features, such as illustrations or initial letters, before
planning the size of lettering and measurements for guide lines.

This Exhibition of
FURNITURE
Will be open to the public Monday
to Friday, from 10 a.m. to 5 p.m.
Admission free

Write out each line separately. Find the *visual* centre and arrange
the lines on a central axis.

This Exhibition of
FURNITURE
Will be open to the public Monday
to Friday, from 10 a.m. to 5 p.m.
Admission free

COME
TO THE
PARTY
on
Saturday
at
my house
JANE

7 p.m.-midnight

Caroline
Invites you
To
Tea
Sunday
June 5th.
2 Porter Rd.
Any time
After 4 p.m.

RSVP
30310

Lines of capital letters only, lines with few ascenders and
descenders, and very short lines which are easily legible, can all be
spaced closer together than $1\frac{1}{2}$ times the x height if desired.
Layouts can be lined up to either left or right margins.

TUESDAY
Link-up

Consider the overall shape and the margins of any layout,
particularly when spacing lines of different sized lettering. Lines
that are too widely spaced lose coherence as a block.

This exercise, which I did as a student, worked out quite well, at the first attempt, for the first ten lines.

I will lift up mine eyes unto the hills
from whence cometh my help. My
help cometh even from the Lord who
hath made Heaven and Earth . He
will not suffer thy foot to be moved
& he that keepeth thee shall not sleep
Behold he that keepeth Israel : shall
neither slumber nor sleep. The Lord
himself is thy keeper the Lord is thy
defence upon thy right hand ; so that

the sun shall not burn thee by day nei
ther the moon by night. The Lord shall
preserve thee from all evil ; yea it is
even he that shall keep thy soul . The
Lord shall preserve thy going out and
thy coming in : from this day forth ev
en forevermore.

The last seven lines need re-arranging. By spacing out the first line and moving the last word or half-word on each line to the beginning of the next, a better shape will be achieved without awkward division of words. 'Even forevermore' can then be written centrally on the last line.

I will lift up mine eyes unto the hills
from whence cometh my help.
My help cometh even from the Lord
who hath made Heaven and Earth .

If it proves necessary to change a text radically, the rough copy should be cut up and re-arranged in a completely different shape. In this case I preferred a more formal arrangement on a central axis.

8 Introducing colour

Contrasts of colour and weight bring lettering to life. Start using colour as soon as you like for titles, initial letters and to stress any important words or phrases. Experiment by cutting up your roughs to judge the different effects of colour against plain text. A pot or block of red poster paint, preferably vermilion, is adequate to start with, cerulean blue and grey also contrast effectively with black or sepia lettering.

A Saxon Song

Tools with the comely names
Mattock and scythe and spade,
Couth and bitter as flames,
Clean, and bowed in the blade,
A man and his tools
Make a man and his trade

Leisurely flocks and herds,
Cool-eyed cattle that come,
Mildly to wonted words
Swine that in orchards roam
A man and his beasts
Make a man and his home

Children sturdy and flaxen
Shouting in brotherly strife,
Like the land they are Saxon,
Sons of a man and his wife,
A man and his loves
Make a man and his life

Poem by V. Sackville West

9 Left-handed calligraphy

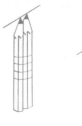

Left oblique writing implements are needed.
Double pencils should be fastened together so
that the line between the two points is at a left
oblique angle. Left oblique round hand nibs
are easily available.

The paper should be to the left of the centre-of-the-body line
and at an optional slant top right to bottom left. The writing
implement should be held in such a way that its shaft is in line with
the forearm. It should not be gripped too near the point. There
should be adequate light coming from the student's right-hand side.

The ease with which a left-hander learns lettering often
depends on the pen hold which has been developed since childhood.
Many left-handers have no trouble at all in writing a Foundational
Hand which is indistinguishable from that of a right-hander.
However, it is very difficult to teach a left-hander who cannot
change an 'over the top' pen hold when the pen can only be
pushed and not pulled downwards. Others find it difficult to get the
pen around to 30° and even more difficult to 45° in order to write
italic script (see p. 40). In this case I suggest they write their own
equivalent of a 'straight pen' or Uncial alphabet as shown on pages
34, 60 and 61. Then when they are more experienced and
consistent letterers a few 30° pencil lines can be drawn on the sheet
to help them change their pen angle.

Left-handers with any problem, whether in handwriting or
lettering, need as free-flowing a writing instrument as possible. So
any of the different makes of broad nibbed fountain or cartridge
pens may help to achieve a freer rhythm. I do not recommend these
pens for regular use, especially for large lettering, as the nibs are
too inflexible, but to help overcome a difficulty or for small
informal writing they can be very useful.

It is difficult to be specific, for the problems of left-handers are
enormously varied. Some of these ideas will help one person and
some another.

Father
Christmas

Written by a 15-year-old student at her first day-school.

Bacchanalian
Dance

Early work by a student who initially had trouble with 30° angle, but solved it, and went on successfully to Formal Italic.

ijlnmhr ace
bold toy vex

This student could produce some good letters but still finds it difficult to produce consistent lettering. She finds an italic fountain pen with left oblique nib helpful.

10 Other basic alphabets

The versatile calligrapher should command a variety of hands. The style, size and weight of the lettering, as well as the colour, can be chosen to fit the character of the subject matter and the mood of the scribe. This is the creative side of calligraphy, using formal writing as an art form. Experienced calligraphers will adapt these basic alphabets, mostly derived from Renaissance writing, to reflect their own individuality. Many develop an informal italic hand for general use. Others, like myself, use a quick upright compressed hand, always returning to the classic hands when formality is required.

The alphabets that follow are: Two variations on the Foundational Hand, Compressed, 'Gothic', Cursive and informal italic. Each has its own distinctive pattern and different uses.

abccdefghijklmnopqrsstuvwxyz &

A compressed alphabet written for me by M. C. Oliver when I was a student

The compressed hand is easy to learn. The small letters are just a narrow version of those of the Foundational Hand and the same capital letters are used. Capitals should not be compressed unless it is essential to fit them into a limited space.

This is a useful rather than a decorative hand. Its even pattern, helped by firm bases to the letters, makes long passages of lettering easily legible. Being narrow, it is more economical and easier to space.

Your Royal Highness

The term *italic* is used to define a sloping, or compressed letter. 'Formal italic' is a large version where, because of its size, the serifs and bases need careful attention. It is most suitable for headings or short passages of text.

32

Dirty British coaster with a salt-stained smoke-stack.

The 'Gothic' hand is slightly slanting and graceful, most suitable for poetry and decorative headings.

The pointed letters barely rest on the lines, making a spirited but not easily legible pattern. The vigorous, more angular capital letters lend themselves to flourishing, once their rather tricky slender forms have been mastered.

As lettering gets smaller and less formal, it must be simplified. Serifs are reduced to flicks, and bases of the first strokes of r, n, h and k, and the first two strokes of m, are omitted in the interest of speed and legibility. Eventually all finishing strokes disappear in fast cursive writing. Students will soon evolve personal styles of informal lettering.

with the field red and the cross & lions silver: has been found. it is said, as the until 1835 was exercised by the occupants of the see "Hoadly of the Church"

The monks and Bishop of Lindisfarne fled with the

Informal italic is useful wherever a lot of information needs to be fitted, decoratively, into a small space, as in this example where it contrasts effectively with a line of compressed writing.

and Alice met and talked and played games together, and the dream world. Outside the Parlour is the Red King asleep and dreaming about YOU!

Use cursive writing where speed and clarity are needed without formality, as in this detail from a panel for an exhibition.

The pen flows and is not always lifted between each stroke. It is easy to write but must be well controlled to produce an even, legible pattern.

Small Roman

CAPITAL LETTERS
D N M K B

With Square Serifs

This has the same round letter form but uses square or slab serifs
and is sometimes called the *Small Roman Alphabet*.

straight
pen
CAPITAL

serif

Written with the pen held straight instead of at a slant of 30°

uncial mxt efw

These letters are sometimes known as *Modern Half Uncials* and are
based on letter forms used in manuscripts written between the 7th
and 10th centuries, such as *The Book of Kells*. (See p. 60.)

Capital letters, ascenders and descenders $1\frac{1}{2}$ x height

abcdefghijklmno
pqrstuvwxyz

Use Foundational Hand capital letters with compressed small letters.

iljmnrhu

Practise these letters first to get an even degree of compression.

oceagbdpq

When round letters are compressed their sides are flattened.

vwxyzsk ft

The diagonal stroke is at a steeper angle when letters are compressed.

Italic letter forms

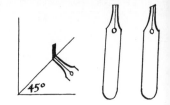

45°

When writing all italic hands the pen is held at 45° to the guide lines. For large formal italic use round hand nibs. For small informal italic there are special italic nibs for right- and left-handers. Guide lines are spaced 5 pen widths apart. Using the same sized nib with differently spaced guide lines and a more sharply angled nib considerably alters the weight of the letter.
Compare the different weight and shape, axis and angle of arches and o's, and the changing angle of the diagonal strokes in:

1 Foundational
2 Compressed
3 Formal italic, and
4 Gothic hands

Formal italic sequences

The arch branches from halfway up the stem of the letter.

Guide lines 5 pen widths apart

x height

Capital letters, ascenders and descenders 1½–2 'x' height

abcdefghijklmn
opqrstuvwxyz

ABCDEFGHIJ
KLMNOPQR
STUVWXYZ

This italic alphabet is written at a 5° slant. It may be helpful for a
beginner to rule a few pencil lines to keep the lettering at a
constant angle – as well as checking the pen angle of 45° from time
to time.

37

'Gothic' hand

x height

Guide lines 5 pen widths apart

Capital letters, ascenders and descenders 1½–2 x height

abcdefghijklm

nopqrstuvwxyz

This might be more accurately described as pointed italic.

&cod ABCD

EJGHIJKL

MNOPQRS

TUVWXYZ

38

Aucassin & Nicolete

Translated *from a 15*. *Anonymous Provencal Ballad. R. Waley scripsit 1950*

Who would list to the good lay
 Gladness of the captive grey?
'Tis how two young lovers met,
 Aucassin and Nicolete,
Of the pains the Lover bore
 And the sorrows he outwore,
For the goodness and the grace,
 Of his love so fair of face

Sweet the song, the story sweet,
 There is no man hearkens it,
No man living 'neath the sun,
 So outwearied, so fordone,
Sick and woful, worn and sad,
 But is healed, but is glad
  'Tis so sweet.

So say they, speak they, tell they the tale

Guide lines approximately 5 pen widths apart

A bpx ⸨

Capital letters, ascenders and descenders 1½–2 x height

The surface of the paper makes so much difference to the weight of very small lettering that it is usually better to gauge the letter-height by eye.

abcdefghijklmnopqrstuvwxyz

Simplest form

A B C D E F G H I J K L M N O
P Q R S T U V W X Y Z &

Alternatives   *1. behold*   *2. behold*

The first variation is a flick serif

Another variation is a forward stroke
added to the top of each ascender except
the letter 'd' which slopes backwards⸗

minimum   Exercises to develop a rhythm when writing informal hands   *ijlnmrhu*
mvmwmxmymzmsmfmt
momcmemamgmbmdmpmq

x height ⁍ four-seven ⁍ x height

Capital letters, ascenders and descenders 1½–2 x height

abcdefghijklmnopqrstuvwxyz

ABCDEFGHIJKLMNOP
QRSTUVWXYZ &

Cursive writing is plain but free. It
is joined-up and faster to write.

The faster these hands are written, the more
the writers individuality will show.
The borderline between informal lettering
and handwriting is difficult to define

When evolving a personal italic hand it is more rewarding, whenever possible, to go back to the original manuscripts rather than to study only from derivative forms.

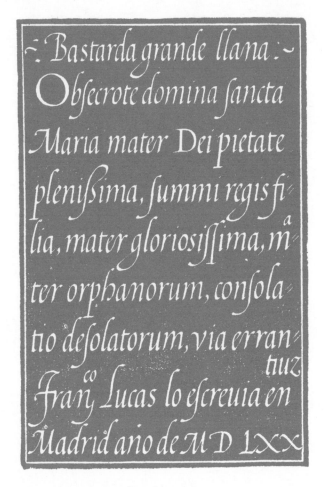

A page from *Arte de escrevir* by Francisco Lucas, a writing-book with woodcuts of scripts printed in Spain in 1577. (Victoria and Albert Museum. Crown Copyright.)

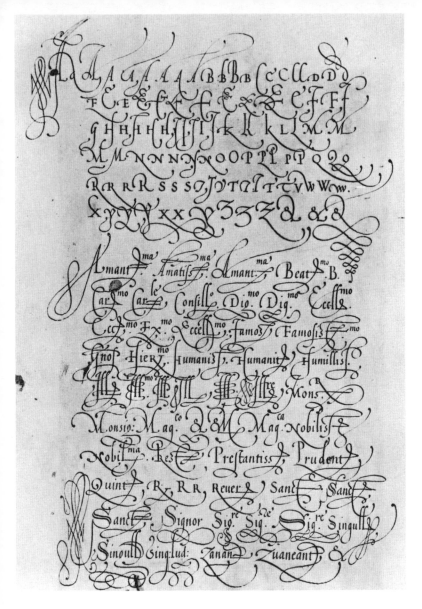

Page from a manuscript written on vellum by Francesco Moro in Italy, about 1560–70 (Victoria and Albert Museum. Crown Copyright.)

Versals *Capital letters built up with a pen*

Versals is the name given to the written capital letters of the
medieval scribes, derived from the incised letters found in Roman
inscriptions (see frontispiece)
Use a fairly narrow nib to outline the letters, giving the uprights a
slightly waisted appearance. Use the full width of the pen for the
double strokes and single cross-strokes,
with the hairline used only for serifs.
Flood the letters with a firm third
stroke of the pen.

ABCDEFGH

Wide letters: O C D G Q M W. Medium letters: H U A N T V.

IJKLMNOP

Narrow letters: I J B E F K L P R S X Y Z.

QRSTUVW

XYZ

Uncial forms

ðeghkƭɯ

CIRCUMSCRIBING

All upright strokes must radiate from the centre of the circle

REVERSED

INFORMAL AND OPEN

Initial letters look better in a contrasting colour.

Praise

In the

Open

Also

1

E there
ven
the
before

2

O that
ne
at
how

3

Versals can be set: 1 Outside the text, 2 Inside the text, 3 Half in and half outside the text
When outside, the text letters should be centred on a perpendicular line.

Initial letters can be given extra weight with a background of colour or pattern, either fitting the shape of the letter or making a rectangle around it.

45

11 Combining different hands

Having mastered a variety of hands, and bearing in mind their special uses and limitations, the calligrapher must next consider contrast of weight and colour. This can be achieved by using different sizes of the same hand, as shown below in the Golf Club notice or in any combination of capital letters, small letters and different alphabets.

Knole Park
Ladies' Golf Club
Hole In One
Name   Hole   Length   Date
Mrs H C Mumford   5th   123yds   4-5-50

    Any sizable block of text (as on pages 50–51) should be completed first, without interruption if possible, as even a short break can cause a noticeable change in the angle or weight of the lettering. Then rough copies of any headings, illustrations or smaller blocks of text should be cut up and laid on the finished work to judge the final weight and spacing. Not only does one's own lettering vary from day to day, but the change from a layout on practise paper to finished work on vellum or handmade paper can completely alter the weight and balance of the design.

    It is an interesting exercise to letter, and then compare, the same text in different layouts, sizes, colours or combinations of hands.

Wrapping Material
supplied by
Waxed-Papers Ltd
Factories at Peckham S.E.15. Merton S.W.9
and Johannesburg S.A.

A notice for a trade fair written in dark red on grey

nor this alone, they give new views to life and teach
THIS BOOK BELONGS TO
Jane Scott
10 HOPE ST. LINCOLN
grieved, the stubborn they chastise, fools they admonish

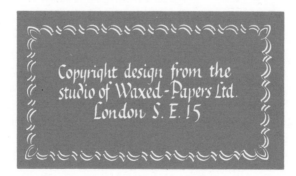

Copyright design from the
studio of Waxed-Papers Ltd.
London S.E.15

A border of wording or pattern can be very effective.

Circular or rectangular designs, with or without illustrations, are decorative and offer very good practice at a relatively early stage. Spirals can be freely written with the help of a flexible rule, or constructed geometrically. Writing can read continuously round the shape or be reversed halfway for easier legibility.

Tongue Twisters

An easy and effective way of using contrasts of size, style and colour, if desired, to produce an interesting layout. This one-colour birthday design would make an unusual card or all-over repeat for packaging.

In this leaving card, designed for someone retiring from publishing, all-over lettering solved the problem of how to fit numerous titles, decoratively, into a limited space.
A 'scroll' nib used for the open lettering, double-pointed, works on the same principle as a double pencil.

THE BOROUGH OF TELSTON

At a meeting of the Council of the Borough of Telston on tenth day of June 1940, held in the Guildhall of the said borough, his Worship the Mayor presiding, it was unanimously decided that this Council do hereby confer upon

Sir John Fenter

The Freedom of the Borough of Telston The most honoured distinction which it is their privilege to bestow in recognition of the services that he has rendered to his borough and county during the twenty five years which he has held office as a councillor of the Borough of Telston. We record with gratitude his tenour of office and his unceasing efforts to further the cause of the under privileged. His constant helpfulness, thoughtfulness and understanding have endeared him to the many citizens of Telston who have benefitted from his advice & assistance, and his fellow members of the Council, who look forward to his guidance for many years to come

Presented to Sir John Fenter with an inscribed piece of silver, by His Worship the Mayor at a ceremony in the Guildhall of Telston on the ninth day of September 1940

The versals and name are in red, small italics in grey and the coat of arms in blue, black and red.

50

A PRAYER FOUND IN
CHESTER CATHEDRAL

Give me a good digestion. Lord.
And also something to digest:
Give me a healthy body. Lord.
And sense to keep it at its best.
Give me a healthy mind.good Lord.
To keep the good and pure in sight:
Which seeing sin is not appalled
But finds a way to set it right.

Give me a mind that is not bored.
That does not whimper.whine or sigh:
Don't let me worry overmuch
About the fussy thing called "I."
Give me a sense of humour. Lord:
Give me the grace to see a joke:
To get some happiness from life
And pass it on to other folk .

The cathedral church of Christ & the Virgin Mary stand within the city walls
on an ancient site In 1093 Hugh Lupus,earl of Chester richly endowed the foundation as a Benedictine monastery. Chester was erected into a bishopric by Henry VIII
in 1541.the church of the dissolved abbey of St Werburgh becoming the cathedral.

12 Flourishes

Use only the inner edge of the nib when finishing a stroke, either
flicking downwards or freely drawing up and over.

Line endings

Ascending strokes

Descending strokes

upper puppy ugly

52

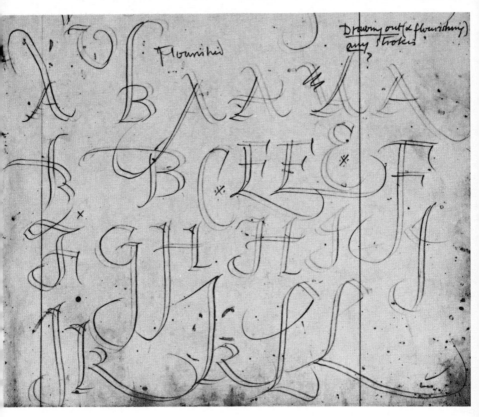

Flourished double-pencil capital letters by Edward Johnston.
Reproduced by kind permission of Dorothy Mahoney.

Use flourishes sparingly
for greatest impact.
Flourished headings or
monograms need careful
designing, making sure
that when extending any
stroke of a letter, it is
enhancing the letter
form, not distorting it.

Flourishes: words and patterns

To add height and weight   to headings

Pen-written pattern adds colour and weight to the bottom of a layout. This example was used on a civic scroll for Sevenoaks.

Repeating patterns based on flourished letters, such as this letter F, are good practise and make decorative endpapers or bookcovers.

Monograms can make interesting personalized stationery. This tree-shaped flourish was designed as a letter-heading for an interior decorator.

One of the key lines of this poem is:
'*A Lillee of a Day is fairer farre in May.*'
The heading was in cerulean blue with
the text in sepia. This was lettered
as a memorial for a friend's child.

The Burne
by *Ben Jonson*

So
Her Most Gracious Majesty
Queen Elizabeth the Second
and
His Royal Highness
Prince Philip Duke of Edinburgh

Heading for a loyal Address in the Silver Jubilee Year
Ornamentation is not always needed; plain, dignified lettering is
suitable even for the most ceremonial occasions. At other times one
can be more imaginative:
this heading for a
presentation poem
was written
in green.

The
Green-sailed Vessel

56

To make Incke

Le Conseil Municipal d'Edenbridge

envoie ses meilleures salutations à ses amis de

Mont Saint Aignan

These three headings were all written in red for use with predominantly black text.

The Charter

13 Materials for more advanced work

Better equipment and materials are needed to achieve a really high standard of calligraphy. A hinged board on an adjustable base, or an architect's table, to ensure steady support at any angle is essential.

For presentation lettering the quality of the actual paper is obviously important. A parchment coloured paper may prove more sympathetic than dead white (and may be less apt to discolour with age) and a deckle edge can often lend distinction to the finished work. A handmade paper is best, but this is increasingly difficult to find, and expensive too. Surfaces vary from smooth 'Hotpress' to more textured 'Not' papers, the weight of the paper again affecting its writing properties. Some may prove especially good for fine writing, others for larger work. It is often a matter of personal preference whether to use a smooth paper or one with more 'tooth' or resistance to the pen.

Experiment also with good machine- and mould-made papers. Smooth, laid or textured papers all prove their worth for different purposes. I have used at least six different types of paper while preparing the lettering for this book.

Chinese or Indian stick ink, freshly rubbed down for use in a slanting palette, makes a free-flowing black. When not too dense, it tends to dry darker at the base of each stroke, giving an interesting balance to a line of lettering.

Artist-quality watercolour, in a tube or pan, is probably the best for fine work. A tube is more convenient to use, but the pigment dries more slowly than that from a pan. Scarlet vermilion, cerulean blue mixed with a little ultramarine, and viridian green are the nearest modern equivalents to the heraldic colours *gules*, *azure* and *vert*.

The traditional natural materials, vellum and quills, produce incomparable results in skilled hands. However, vellum is difficult and expensive to obtain, and needs special care in preparation, stretching or framing. Quills require careful selection, drying and cutting, and constant trimming during use. They are counter-productive if not correctly used.

Family tree written in red, black and gold on vellum.

Gilding – the laying of size and gold leaf which is then burnished – is best carried out on vellum, and again is a complicated procedure. There are several commercial preparations that can be applied with a brush onto paper; these can be quite effective if used sparingly.

Heraldry is a fascinating and complex study. Coats of arms and heraldic creatures or devices may be used wherever appropriate as ornament to calligraphic texts but great care must be taken to be accurate both in the drawing and colouring.

It is not possible to cover these advanced techniques in a relatively short book. For further information students should refer to *Writing and Illuminating and Lettering* by Edward Johnston.

14 Studying and using historical hands

When approaching a new alphabet or passage from a manuscript that you wish to study or copy, divide the letters into sequences of those comprising the same strokes. This way you will quickly learn their special characteristics and become consistent in copying or adapting them to your own needs. The letter sequences may vary from one alphabet to another, and there are usually several letters that bear no stroke resemblance to the others.

An alphabet should, where possible, be chosen to suit the language of the text. Classic Roman letters may look inappropriate for a Celtic name, and a German text seems to look better in traditional Black letter, which suggests that there is probably a visual association of language to letter in most people's minds and that some languages look better when written in the hands evolved for them.

Since writing is as much a legacy of the past as architecture or painting, I find that using the styles and tools of a different age gives me an insight into the period.

Uncials

An example of Irish Half Uncial from *The Book of Kells*.
Trinity College, Dublin.

Double pencil uncial capital letters by Edward Johnston.
Reproduced by kind permission of Dorothy Mahoney.

ABCDEFGhijklmNOpq
RSTUVWXYZ abcdefghijk
lmnopqrstuvwxyz

Modern half-uncial alphabet written out for a student by Edward
Johnston, *c.* 1930
These letters are written with a straight pen.

1FOR EVANS

From a retirement scroll written by the author.

iljrnmhuyvw

ceoabpqgd

tfɪskʒ

A simplified Gothic or black letter alphabet
The letters are constructed almost entirely of straight lines.
Spacing is important to produce the characteristic even texture of
Gothic script.
The space between letters should be equivalent to the space
enclosed by each letter.

Aabcdefghijklmnopqrſsſstuvwxyz.&c.
ABCDEFGHJKLMNOP
QRSTUWXYZZJC.

This alphabet appears in *The Universal Penman*, engraved by
George Bickham in 1743.

A a b c d e f g

honneur et
ſeruice a dieu

a b c d e f g h i

Aſſez demande
qui bien ſert

An elegant Black letter (*Lettre de forme*) and the so-called *Lettre Bastarde*, both from *Champ Fleury* by Geofroy Tory.

Capital letters by Geofroy Tory. From *Champ Fleury*, 1529.
Not all of these forceful capital letters are immediately legible
today; but those used for these honey-jar labels needed no
attention, although I simplified the small letters considerably.

so proṇe aṇd ready to labour as hit hath beṇ, aṇd that age crepeth oṇ ṃe dayly aṇd febleth all the bodye.

Lettering played an important part when I worked with a team of designers on a travelling exhibition of the history of writing and printing. It not only added to the general atmosphere, but by writing the notices and quotations in a simplified, enlarged hand incorporating some of the unfamiliar letterforms of the 15th century, we sought to help the public decipher the original manuscripts on show, many concerned with William Caxton. On tour, simple hand-lettering enabled last-minute alterations to be practical and financially possible.

Postcard for sale at printing exhibition. The larger lettering was written with double fibre-tipped pens and painted in.

for they wende that they wolde haue amended her tatches / ẓ hyr wicked thewes / but of suche condicions they were / that for fayre speche ẓ warnynge, they vpdden al the wers) and for berynges

Early Caxton typeface which resembled his own handwriting

Studying and using historical hands: Copperplate or 'Roundhand'

It takes endless practice to develop a good copybook
or copperplate hand. The technique is different from that of
present-day handwriting or lettering with a broad-nibbed
pen. Differing pressure on the fine flexible nib makes the
thick and thin strokes. In the extremely controlled letters the
downstroke is heavy and the upstroke thin, the arches and often
unfamiliar ligatures are rounded and very finely written.
In decoration the weights of the strokes are changed at will.

The Victorian copybook method of repetition of a short
saying is the best way of developing a regular hand.

Health is valuable

Health is valuable

Gaming is a wicked cust

Gaming is a wicked cust

Excerpts from two pages of a copybook written by Joseph Wilkes
in 1840 when aged 14 years (Reproduced by kind permission of his
great-granddaughter, Anne Isobel Jackson). Copperplate writing
evolved as people tried to copy with their pens the controlled but
flowing strokes of the copper engraver's burin.

Aim at improvement in every line.

Businefs makes a Man respected.

Commendation animates the mind.

W. Clark scrip.

The difference between these two illustrations is that John Wilkes's work is photographed from his original copybook writing with its extremely fine, sometimes broken hairlines, not easy to reproduce but nonetheless much closer to the effect that students will be able to reproduce by their own efforts.

The William Clark example was reproduced by being engraved by George Bickham and it appeared in 1743 in his book *The Universal Penman* (a facsimile of which has been printed by Dover Publications). Engraving produces a more continuous and even fine line than is possible with a pen.

Studying and using historical hands: Copperplate or 'Roundhand'

This enlarged alphabet is useful because it shows the construction of the letters.

From a Copy Book Written for the Use of the Young Gentlemen at the Academy in Greenwich. By Thomas Weston, 1726.

How to construct a flourish
By Edward Cocker from *Magnum in Parvo or, the Pen's Perfection*, 1672 (both Victoria and Albert Museum. Crown Copyright)

There are special nibs made for copperplate
writing, though they are probably not as flexible
as their Victorian ancestors or a finely cut quill.

I used copperplate extensively in an exhibition about Lewis
Carroll, both small writing and a quick large version for display
purposes. Recently I was asked to write a passage from John
Clare's work for an educational book. The heading is reproduced
by kind permission of Hodder and Stoughton Educational.

Hanks

Larger lettering, where the letters are outlined with a thin drawing
nib and filled in by brush, is usually referred to as script lettering,
and is extremely useful to a designer. An excellent reference book is
Tommy Thompson's Script Lettering for Artists.

Adlam Burnett
Goudhurst

This nameplate was designed for the makers of fine keyboard
instruments

half an inch

equals $4\frac{1}{2}$ times size o, the largest round hand nib. If you want to produce larger lettering using the same letterforms, correctly proportioned, other implements must be explored.

Various large nibs which are meant for poster work, are available. However, broad metal nibs tend to be rigid, and it is difficult to produce really good lettering with them. They are best used only when simple non-serif letters are required.

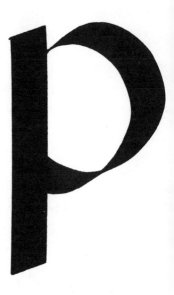

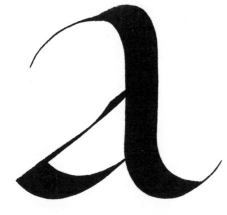

Thin balsa wood cuts easily to make a large flexible writing tool. This letter was written with a pen made from the side of a match-box. It was cut across the grain with a sharp pair of scissors and wedged into a soft stick for a handle then dipped in ink.

These rectangular-leaded pencils are very useful for quick notices, and can produce excellent results when skillfully used. They need careful and frequent sharpening of all five planes of the lead. Finished work must be sprayed with fixative.

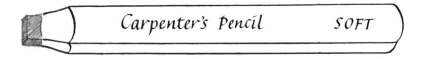

Carpenter's Pencil   *SOFT*

They can be cut down in size
and look very effective when used on textured coloured paper

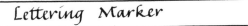

Lettering Marker

A wedge shaped fibre tipped pen is also useful.

Pens can be strapped together and used like double pencils
Measure $4\frac{1}{2}$ times the distance between points for correct letter size

Can be written fairly freely and large with felt or fibre-tipped pens.
They can be filled in or left

Double letters

Double letters can be constructed to enlarge the scale still further, using two strokes for thick lines and one for thin.

reduced

double

Can be even larger still

Brush Letters

develop quite naturally from pen lettering

Letterforms

of the

foundational

hand

can be produced just as easily with a brush

a Character Script

can be evolved to suit any subject or mood.

74

Use a good quality medium-sized brush.

Vary
in size

Thick
or
thin

and shape

To suit subject and layout

round
and
Square

Letters are formed by varying the pressure and amount of ink on the brush.

Speed
and
Freedom

are the advantages
of brush scripts

Fat

Baby

dry

An Announcement

MADE IN ENGLAND

closed

Free

open

Flowers

Congratulations

Sale
Sale
Sale
Sale
Sale
Sale
Today

Greetings

Advertising

Wrap fresh food in foil

Birkett's
Milk Loaf

17 Preparing work for reproduction

Preparing lettering specifically for reproduction poses certain problems for the calligrapher. These can usually be overcome, provided that one has enough information before starting work. For instance, it is important to know whether the lettering will be reproduced in the same size or in a reduced version. Reduction can help to eliminate roughness or unevenness, but it can also show up faults in spacing, and it is often difficult to judge the effect in advance. Viewing the work through a reducing glass helps one to spot such faults before the work is submitted. Remember that when pen lettering is reduced, the thin strokes made by the edge of the nib, which remain the same however thick the width of the pen, will become very thin indeed and may disappear altogether if the reduction is too great. I usually like to work about one-half up for reproduction but nearly all the pages which were specially prepared for this book were written to the same size.

The nuances of texture which add interest and beauty to an original piece of calligraphy are invariably lost in reproduction, so there is no point in using expensive paper or vellum. The best results are achieved by working on a smooth white paper (not card or drawing board, as this is not resilient enough) and by using a uniformly black ink. I use a liquid bottled watercolour which flows easily but is very dense. Unfortunately this cannot easily be touched up since it is non-waterproof, so if corrections are anticipated it is best in this one instance to use waterproof ink.

In cases where the lettering is to appear white on a black ground, which can be very effective for certain types of work, it is much easier to work in black on white paper rather than attempting to use white paint. The result can then be photo-graphically reversed. When working in this way, it is important that the hair lines do not become too thin and risk closing up.

When more than one colour is to be used, it may be more economical for your client if you do this on a transparent overlay (using a special transparent film or thick tracing paper) or by a keyed drawing, making the separation yourself rather than leaving it to the printer. If in doubt, always seek advice.

Chatham Vellum represents the result of a five year research programme. It is made entirely from raw flax - the fibre from which linen is woven and which was the very foundation of European paper-making for centuries. We have combined this with an advanced sizing system which results in an acid-free paper with first class writing properties.

Four deckle edges and the delightful flaxen tone which is entirely natural - no colours are added - combine to give a character suitable for the finest work.

Full details are given overleaf

·The inside is blank for you to test

Chatham Vellum

Hand-made Calligraphy Paper from Barcham Green

A brochure for a paper manufacturer. The original was lettered one half up.

18 Calligraphy at work

The examples on the following pages show some of the many practical uses for calligraphy.

Cards for all occasions

These simple designs can be lettered in one or two colours, or more carefully prepared as finished drawings for reproduction.

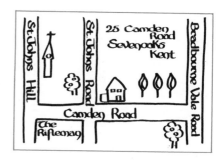

Some first-year students' cards

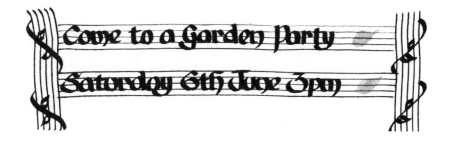

ааааааааааааааааааа

A Precious Oyntment for all Manner of Aches

Take a pound waight of Sage, as much
Rew, half a pound of Wormewood
and as much Crops of Bayes, &
beat them very small in a Morter
Take two pound and a halfe of
Sheepes Tallow & temper it with
the hearbes that be beaten, put in
a can & set them on the hot embers
Put thereto a Pottle of Oyle of
Olife and let it stand upon the
Embers two houres and a halfe
at the least, then strain it
through a course cloath and
put it in an earthen pot & so
occupie it. This would be made
in May or June.

From
The Widdowes Treasure

1595

Jan. 21st.   Feb. 19th

aquarius   the water carrier

Zodiac birthday card. Lino-cut by Pat Savage, printed in black
with cerulean blue lettering.

Left. Quick sketch for a 'Get well soon' card.
In this case it is the content, not the design, that provides the
interest.

Film titles
These were lettered in white
on a dark blue ground and
touched up with a brush.
Reproduced by permission of
Matthew Nathan.

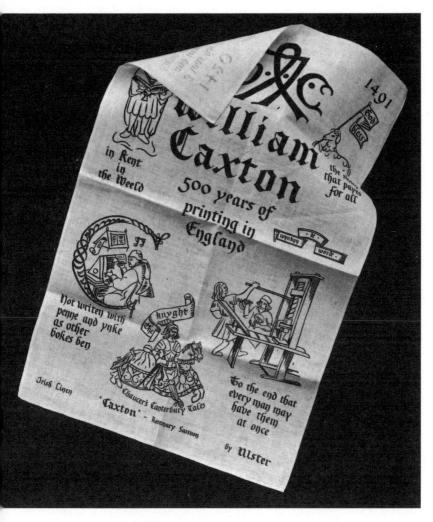

Tea towel printed in black on linen by the Ulster Weaving Company Ltd. This was designed for the Caxton exhibition (see p. 65).

(see p. 65).

Lettering can be used effectively in textile design, smoother material obviously being more suitable for smaller lettering.

Peacock

Research in the British Library provided eight different 16th- and 17th-century recipes from early cookery books for use on large table-mats and their accompanying coasters. Printed in sepia on parchment coloured paper.

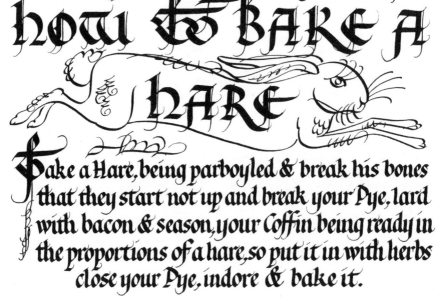

From a 17th. English Recipe

how to BAKE A hare

Take a Hare, being parboyled & break his bones that they start not up and break your Pye, lard with bacon & season, your Coffin being ready in the proportions of a hare, so put it in with herbs close your Pye, indore & bake it.

Thyme

Thymus Durius

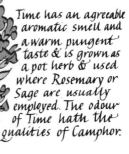

There be two sorts of Garden Time among the old writers, the latter Herbarists have found more. Thymus Durius, or Common Garden Time is so well known that it needeth no description.

Time has an agreeable aromatic smell and a warm pungent taste & is grown as a pot herb & used where Rosemary or Sage are usually employed. The odour of Time hath the qualities of Camphor.

Time boiled in water and honie, and drunken is good against the cough & shortness of breath

From a set of eight different 'herbal lore' designs printed in colour. All these were made into mats by Lady Clare Ltd, Lutterworth, Rugby.

Camomile

Anthemis Nobilis

Calendar

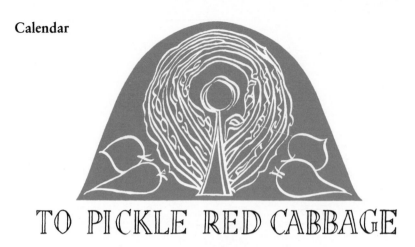

The finished drawings for the illustrations were worked in white on a black ground and the strokes were then thickened where necessary to allow for the slight narrowing that would occur during letterpress printing. Each page was printed in an appropriate colour and black.

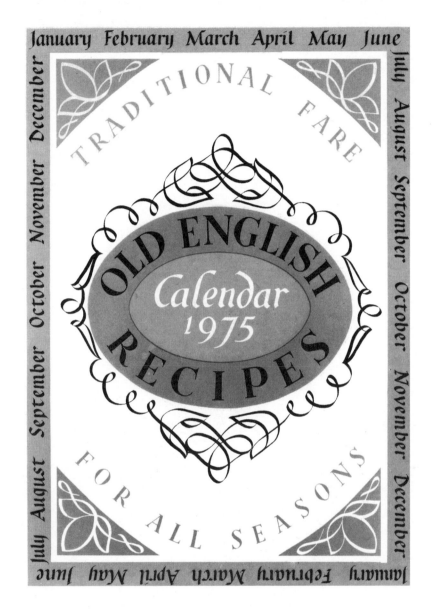

Cover printed in red, black and gold.
Reproduced by kind permission of J. Salmon Ltd.

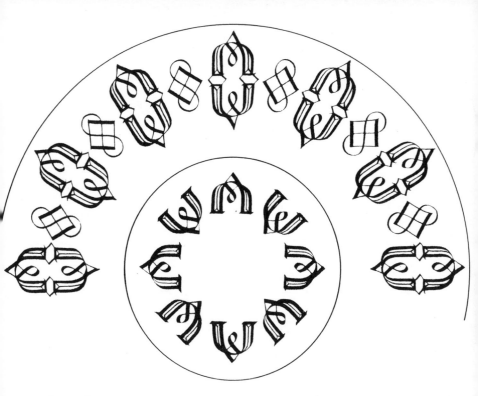

Calligraphic patterns
Mat designs. Reproduced by kind permission of John Lewis
Partnership.

There were three large and three small designs. The small ones used
simplified versions of the same shapes rather than reductions.
Finished drawings were worked 1½ times size. Geometrically
measured and marked out and the pattern traced down, the
drawing was rotated as each segment was completed.

Repeating patterns

A single motif, either of pattern or words, can be repeated to form
an effective all-over design for use on textiles or paper products.

TO ROAST A PIGGE
From an Elizabethan recipe

Take your Pigge and draw it, wash it cleane and take out the liver. Perboile it and straine it with a little creame and yolkes of egges, put these to grated bread, marrow and small raisons, nutmegs in powder, mace, ginger & salt, sturre all these together, put into the Pigges bellye, sowe it then spit it with the haire on. When it is halfe enough pull off the skinne, baste it, and when it is enough crumb it with white bread, sugar, sinamon and ginger, let it be somewhat browne and so serve it.

TO SEETHE A CARPE
From a 17th Century Recipe

Fyrste take a Carpe, boile it in water & salt then take of the broth, put in a pot and put thereto as much wine as there is broth, with Rosemary, Parslie, Time, Marjoram, bounde together, put thereto as much of sliced onyons, small raisons, whole Maces, a dish of butter and a little sugar so that it be not too sharpe or too sweete, and let all these seethe together If the wine be not sharpe enough then put thereto a little vinegar. And so serve it upon soppes with the brothe.

Your Crabs being boyled, take the meat out of the bodies and barrels and save the great claws and small legs whole to garnish your dish. Strain the meat with some Claret wine, grated Bread, Mace, Nutmeg Salt and Butter, stew them together for one quarter of an hour on a soft fire in a Pipkin, and being stewed almost dry, put in an egg yolk with the juice of several Oranges, beat up thick, and put the meat in shells. Dish the legs round about & serve.

To make A PARTRIDGE TART
From a 17th Century recipe

Take the flesh of four or five Partridges and mince them very fine with the same weight of Beef marrow as you have of Partridge flesh, two ounces of Orangeadoes & green Citron minced together as small as your meat, and season with Cloves, Mace, Nutmeg, a little Salt and Sugar. Mix them all together and bake in a Puffe Paste When it is baked, put in half a graine of Muske or Amber brayed in a Morter or Dishe and a spoonful of Rosewater & Orange juice and so serve it up

TO STEW CRABS
From a recipe written in 1605

Repeating design for a wrapping paper. By permission of Brown, Knight and Truscott Ltd.

93

The aim of this book has been to give the beginner who is prepared to persevere a grounding in the basic skills of pen and brush lettering and to suggest ways in which these can be developed and used.

I hope it may also have suggested how the study of calligraphy can increase one's awareness of the relationship between the words, whether prose or poetry, and the manner in which they are written. This is something which is difficult to explain or teach. One can only say that the ability of the trained hand to put on paper the image in the mind's eye – sometimes with results which may surprise the creator – and the insight this can give one into the meaning of the text are among the rewards which can come as a result of practice and self criticism, both of which are essential for the committed calligrapher.

I should like to think that the historical examples I have included will encourage some people to look more deeply into the fascinating history of writing. Manuscripts are all around us; in museums, libraries, local archives and churches, perhaps even in our own attics. The letter forms which surround us on all sides, whether written, carved or printed, influence our lives at every level; the road signs which direct us, the typeface of the books or newspapers we read every day, the graphics on the television screen and the lettering on packaging or advertising which helps to sway our choice.

There need be no artificial divisions among these varied forms of lettering. Each has its own function and usefulness. The study and enjoyment of them can teach us a great deal and help us to widen our horizons.

approximate Ratios

alt. 30° · alt.
alt 4 NW.

Ratios Constant in practice

abcde

approx Spacing 3 os

fghijk

lmnopqrstuvw

R

www x y y z   Hyerosolomiae
Ieros

& &   1 2 3 4 6 8 5 7 9 0   1 7 9 0

1 2 3 3 4 5 6 7 8 9 0   K

ABC ABCDEFGHI
CB (I) JKKKLMN

for Mimi Bishop 7 Feb. 1927

Acknowledgments

My acknowledgments must start with Geoffrey Holden and the late M. C. Oliver, who trained me as a scribe. Then I would like to thank Esther Aresty, who first suggested that I should write this book, and Jean Ellsmoor, who saw to it that I did; Joyce Whalley and Dorothy Mahoney, for their help and encouragement; the manufacturers and others who have allowed me to reproduce work which I have done for them; the many students who tested my teaching method; and finally my husband, John, who has long suffered from a paper-strewn home and who has spent a lot of time correcting my grammar.